A Brief Memoir of *Elizabeth Fry* (1781–1845)

Edited by David Goff

Friends United Press
Richmond, Indiana • www.fum.org/shop

A *Brief Memoir of Elizabeth Fry* orginally published by the Association of Friends for the Diffusion of Religious and Useful Knowledge, Philadelphia, Pennsylvania, 1858.

Copyright © 2008 by David Goff

All rights reserved. No portion of this book may be reproduced, stored in electronic retrieval system or transmitted in any form or by means—electronic, mechanical, photocopy, recording or other—except for brief quotations in printed reviews, without the prior permission of the publisher.

Friends United Press
101 Quaker Hill Drive
Richmond IN 47374
friendspress@fum.org
www.fum.org/shop

Cover art from engraving of "Mrs. Fry Reading to the Prisoners in Newgate, in the year 1816." Religious Society of Friends, England.

Library of Congress Cataloging-in-Publication Data

A brief memoir of Elizabeth Fry / edited by David Goff.
   p. cm.
  Originally published: Philadelphia : New York : Association of Friends for the Diffusion of Religious and Useful Knowledge, [1858]
  ISBN-13: 978-0-944350-74-4 (pbk.)
  1. Fry, Elizabeth Gurney, 1780-1845. 2. Prison reformers--Great Britain--Biography. 3. Quakers--Great Britain--Biography. I. Goff, David.
  HV8978.F7E55 2008
  365'.7092--dc22
  [B]
                              2008018304

Original Note

This little volume is reprinted from one of the publications of the London Tract Association of Friends with a few unimportant changes and the addition of some passages taken from an obituary in the *Annual Monitor*.

Editor's Note on Friends United Press Edition

This work is being republished with the intention of making the life and writings of Elizabeth Fry accessible to readers in the twenty-first century. A work of this nature is very much in order as most modern readers, even among Friends, know little to nothing of the history of this eighteenth century Quaker, her life of ministry, and her struggles in the work of prison reform. It is hoped that by seeing a glimpse of her life in this small book that the reader will be motivated to read one of the longer works identified in the bibliography. The primary editorial principle being clarity for the modern reader, three changes appear in this text: spelling, grammar, and punctuation have been updated in accordance with modern American usage; the polished, sometimes stilted rhetorical style has been modified to conform more closely to modern tastes; and much of the religious jargon and/or Quaker terminology which may be unclear to the modern reader has been either changed or explained. At the same time, every attempt has been made to maintain the general tone, style, and voice of the anonymous author. Unless otherwise noted, direct quotes from Elizabeth are from the two-volume *Memoir of the Life of Elizabeth Fry* (1847), which includes large portions of her journal and is edited by her daughters, Katharine Fry and Rachel Elizabeth Cresswell. These are cited by volume and page number. Direct quotes from Elizabeth are not edited unless otherwise noted. References have been added for Bible quotations.

Introductory Encomium

[Editor's note: In the original text, this stood at the beginning of chapter 1, but makes more sense from our modern perspective as an introductory page.]

On the page of divine inspiration is written the words, "The righteous will be remembered forever" (Ps. 112:6). This has, doubtless, a special reference to that "witness [which] is in heaven," that "record . . . upon high" (Job 16:19) by which the actions of the just are registered in the "book of life" (Rev. 20:12). Yet it also indicates that the bright course of those faithful servants of God and benefactors of mankind, who "rest from their labors," and whose "works do follow them" (Rev. 14:13) is designed to serve as an ensign throughout succeeding generations, exhibiting, by the force of a holy example, the blessedness and the duty of treading in that pathway of Christian dedication, in which they sought to follow him who "went about doing good" (Acts 10:38), and who "came to seek and to save that which was lost" (Luke 19:10). In reviewing the life and character of Elizabeth Fry, in reflecting on the self-sacrificing benevolence which actuated her spirit, and in tracing the deep current of Christian piety from which it sprang, the reader may be animated to seek, like her, to promote the glory of God, and to spread the knowledge of him and of his son, Jesus Christ.

Table of Contents

Introduction: Elizabeth Gurney Fry, A Model of Quaker Ministry 7

Chapter One: The Early Years 17

Chapter Two: A Spiritual Awakening. 21

Chapter Three: Marriage and Early Days of Ministry. 31

Chapter Four: Ministering to those in Prison. 41

Chapter Five: Enlarging the Scope of Prison Ministry 55

Chapter Six: A Union of Christian Effort 63

Chapter Seven: Traveling Ministry 75

Chapter Eight: The Final Year 91

Notes. 97

Bibliography 99

Introduction

Elizabeth Gurney Fry, A Model of Quaker Ministry

Elizabeth Gurney Fry, who lived from the latter years of the eighteenth century through the middle of the nineteenth century, is a fascinating blend of Quaker minister, "bluestocking" reformer, and promoter of ecumenical service ministries. As a minister in the Society of Friends, she faithfully served in the traditional style as a Friend who spoke forth out of the silence of the gathered meeting.[1] Elizabeth worked hand-in-hand with the bluestocking reformers of her day who sought to promote education, care for the poor, and equality under the law, as well as numerous other social reforms. Also, though faithful to her own Quaker heritage, she was able to work in close fellowship with members of other denominations for the propagation of the gospel and for the implementation of such innovative social ministries as prison ministries, abolition societies, and homeless shelters. She was able to move easily in such varied social circles as the English and European nobility, Meetings of the Society of Friends, English political officials, Coast Guard, English fishermen, and death-row felons in the English penal system. She was friends with a variety of distinguished literary figures such as Sir Walter Scott, Mariah Edgeworth, and Joanna Baillie. Elizabeth Gurney Fry was truly an exceptional person and one who made a powerful impact on the society of her time.

Child of the Enlightenment

Elizabeth was the fourth child of John and Catherine Bell Gurney. Both were the descendants of long-established Quaker families. Catherine was descended from Robert Barclay, who was the most highly regarded theologian produced by the Society of Friends prior to the twentieth century. John's family had been Friends since the days of George Fox. The Gurneys, though Quaker from birth and descended from some of the "leading lights" of the early Quaker movement, were not particularly devout. They did not follow the plain dress and plain speech practices of their early Quaker ancestors. Mrs. E.R. Pitman (1886) describes this distinction as follows:

> . . . they were calm, intellectual, benevolent, courteous, and popular people; not so very unlike others, save that they attended "First-day meeting," but differing from their co-religionists in that they abjured the strict garb and the "thee" and "thou" of those who followed George Fox to unfashionable lengths, whilst their children studied music and dancing. (2)

John Gurney was a wealthy wool merchant. When Elizabeth was about six years old he moved his family from Norwich to the family estate at Earlham, just outside of the city. There the eleven Gurney children, girls as well as boys, received an excellent education under the guidance of their mother, though it was not a particularly "Quaker" style of education:

> The education of the young Gurneys was more characteristic of the aristocracy of Norwich than of Quakerism. It included drawing under the instruction of John Crome, later to be famous as one of the founders of the "Norwich School" of landscape painting. It included music and far-ranging reading. By the early 1790s the older sisters . . . were enjoying Rousseau, Paine, and Godwin with free-thinking teenage friends. (Swift 1960, 178)

Though not plain in their dress or speech, the aristocratic Gurneys faithfully attended Goats Lane Meeting in Norwich. The young Elizabeth tended to avoid attending Meeting when she could, however. Tragedy struck the family when Elizabeth was only twelve years old. Mrs. Gurney died and Catherine ("Kitty"), the oldest daughter, stepped into the maternal role to help raise and educate her younger siblings. Despite their loss, the Gurney children grew into happy, healthy adults and were a close-knit and loving family.

Spiritual Awakening

It was Elizabeth's spiritual awakening under the preaching of the American Quaker, William Savery that began a quiet revolution in her family. Just prior to her eighteenth year she and her family attended Meeting at Goats Lane where William Savery was preaching. Savery was following the time-honored practice of the itinerant Quaker minister that had originated with George Fox. Elizabeth experienced a religious conversion under Savery's preaching that led to her "convincement" of the truths of her own Quaker faith.[2] Elizabeth describes this experience in her journal as follows:

> My imagination has been worked upon, and I fear all that I have felt will go off. I fear it now; though at first I was frightened that a plain Quaker should have made so deep an impression on me; but how truly prejudiced in me to think that because good came from a Quaker I should be led away by enthusiasm and folly. But I hope I am now free from such fears. I wish the state of enthusiasm I am in may last, for today I have felt that there is a God; I have been devotional, and my mind has been led away from the follies that it is mostly wrapped up in. We had much serious conversation; in short, what he said and what I felt was like a refreshing shower falling upon earth that had been dried up for ages. It has not made me unhappy: I have felt ever since humble. I have longed for virtue. I hope to be truly virtuous, to let sophistry fly from my mind, not to be enthusiastic and foolish but only to be so far religious as will lead to virtue. (I:36)

From the beginning of the Quaker faith, the emphasis has been on experiential religion. As a result of this encounter, Elizabeth became the living embodiment of the Quaker faith, blending the solid experience and commitment to Quaker principles found in lifelong members with the excitement and enthusiasm of those who had become personally convinced of the reality of the Quaker way. Her testimony and zeal, though initially resisted by the other members of her family, eventually led several of them to walk a similar path. Her brothers and sisters joined her in many of her efforts for the poor and needy, and one brother, Joseph John Gurney, became a powerful Quaker minister in his own right.

An Exceptional Quaker Minister

The Society of Friends came into being under the powerful and outspoken preaching of George Fox, in the middle of the seventeenth century. Fox was attempting to restore primitive (first century) Christianity during the religious conflicts that culminated in the English Civil War. Refusing to side with either Royalists or Puritans, Fox and his followers experienced heavy persecution and imprisonment. Acts of Toleration were eventually passed in the early part of the eighteenth century, allowing Quakers and other dissenting minorities to live in peace. By the middle of the eighteenth century, Quakers were no longer aggressive radicals, but had merged into society. Quaker Meetings had always begun in silence, followed by powerful (and often quite loud) preaching, but in Elizabeth's time many of the Meetings had little or no preaching at all, and were often completely silent.

The founders of the Friends movement would have found in Elizabeth a kindred spirit. As a Quaker, and later as a Quaker minister, Elizabeth would not have seemed as exceptional if she had lived in an earlier time. A quick look at the first generation of Friends reveals a group of people who were willing to suffer imprisonment and death for their principles. Plain dress that scorned ornamentation and plain speech which rejected forms of address that indicated social status were serious issues for these early Friends. They believed in a radical equality and refused to comply with the social practices by which those of lower classes showed respect for their "betters." Rejecting liturgy and religious ritual, early Friends began their Meetings for Worship in silence, waiting on the guidance of the Holy Spirit. They did not often remain silent for long, however. These early Meetings of Friends had much more in common with modern Pentecostal or charismatic meetings than with the staid silent meetings of their descendants. Meetings involved testimonies, inspired (and often lengthy) preaching, and even music.

Jean Hatton (2005) gives a good description of the change that had taken place by the time in which Elizabeth was ministering:

> By the mid-eighteenth century, the Quaker focus was on social exclusivity, on passive contemplation, and a denial of what was outward and "creaturely." The distinctive plain dress, speech and manners that had once seemed so vital a witness became regulated by strict codes, and Quaker opposition to the world was often expressed in a rejection of music, dancing, novels, and plays. Anxieties also increased over distinguishing the divine from the creaturely voice, so that in time, the Meetings that had once been a platform for spoken prayer and testimony became ever more silent. Sometimes several weeks of Meetings might pass without a word being spoken. (48)

It is from these latter times that the common phrase "silent as a Quaker Meeting" is drawn. It certainly does not reflect the earlier, more radical years of Quakerism, nor does it reflect the powerful, though humble, eloquence of Elizabeth Gurney Fry. Living in this time of growing "Quietism" among Friends, Elizabeth was noteworthy as a powerful preacher and a tireless reformer.

Working for Social Justice

Though Elizabeth was an ardent social reformer, particularly in light of her work with prisons, she was neither alone nor unique in her efforts. The eighteenth century was a time of excitement and enthusiasm in England. The Monarchy was stable, the economy was booming, a rising middle class was thriving, education was becoming increasingly more available and important to people of all classes, and there was finally a sense of toleration among the myriad of religious groups who were competing for the attention of the English people.

Though Elizabeth lived a generation after the time of the original Bluestocking Movement, their influence was still felt in the England of her day. Bluestocking feminism provided an avenue for women to be active in promoting their own intellectual development, as well as in education, religion, and social reform. The Bluestocking Movement consisted of groups of women who met socially in their salons to discuss enlightenment ideas and to advocate for women's education and intellectual life. "The name 'bluestocking clubs' was applied to these informal gatherings because one of the regulars, Benjamin Stillingfleet, acknowledged the informal, uncourtly nature of the gatherings by wearing the blue worsted stockings of informal, domestic dress rather than the black silk stockings of formal or courtly social occasions" (Kelly 1995, 16). The earlier influence of the Bluestocking Movement by no means minimizes the efforts of Elizabeth on behalf of the needy, but makes it clear why her ideas were able to catch on so readily.

Of course, as is always the case, there were those who did not agree with her methods and perhaps thought her something of a "busybody." One of the most notable of these was George Gordon, the famous English poet known as Lord Byron. As a "friend of a friend," there is no doubt that Byron had firsthand knowledge of Elizabeth's activities. Byron moved in the same social circles, naming Sir Walter Scott and Joanna Baillie among his acquaintances. He addressed the following lines to her in the Tenth Canto of his famous "Don Juan" (1994):

>Oh Mrs. Fry! Why go to Newgate? Why
>Preach to poor rogues? And wherefore not begin
>With Carlton, or with other houses? Try
>Your head at harden'd and imperial sin.
>To mend the people's an absurdity,
>A jargon, a mere philanthropic din,
>Unless you make their betters better: Fy!
>I thought you had more religion, Mrs. Fry. (773)

Despite the reactions of Byron and others, Elizabeth's approach was successful. She was not only able to touch the lives of individual prisoners, but through her advocacy for systemic change she was able to impact the lives of many who would receive humane treatment as a result of her activities, though might never know her name.

Cooperating with Other Faiths

Elizabeth, though a devout Quaker, did not isolate herself from those of other faiths. Part of her success in her social ministries was related to her willingness to promote an ecumenical approach in ministering to the poor, the prisoners, the enslaved, the homeless, and other suffering members of the society in which she lived. In her mind, social justice was not just a Quaker concern (though Friends had always taken this issue very seriously) but a Christian concern. "[T]he Quaker movement . . . was still very active in the eighteenth century as advocates for such social reforms as nonviolence, an end to slavery, education for all, equal rights for women, and caring for the needs of the poor . . . [and] the social reforms that they had been advocating for almost 100 years had begun to permeate society" (Goff 2004, 11). Elizabeth was gifted with the ability to reach out and work harmoniously with members of other religious denominations and organizations to meet both the spiritual and physical needs of suffering humanity. Many examples of this will be seen in the following *Memoir*, but one example illustrates this quite effectively. In 1811, Elizabeth's brother, Joseph John Gurney, was the moving force behind the organization of a Norwich auxiliary of the British and Foreign Bible Society. Elizabeth attended the organizational meeting held at Earlham. The following account describes the events that took place at this meeting:

> Many persons of learning and piety manifested their approval, and testified to the powerful efficacy of her ministrations. On the day when the Bible Society was established at Norwich in 1811, a large company dined at Earlham Hall; Elizabeth Fry was then on a visit there, and at the table she was surrounded by six clergymen of the Established Church, three dissenting ministers, besides some of the Society of Friends. . . . [At this point, Elizabeth felt power-

fully moved to call for a time of silence, and then to pray audibly out of the silence.] Soon after Elizabeth Fry had taken her seat, a Baptist minister said, "This is an act of worship." A clergyman added, "We want no wine, for there is that amongst us that does instead." The excellent and devoted C. F. Steinkoff then expressed his unity, saying that he felt the Spirit of prayer, although, being a foreigner, he could not understand all the words in which it had been uttered. Another clergyman made some weighty remarks on the manner in which the Almighty visited his people; that neither sex, nor anything else, stood in the way of his grace. (I:173-4)

This is just one of many examples of Elizabeth's ability to break through the barriers of gender discrimination and denominationalism to accomplish common Christian goals.

Gurney Endeavors

The Gurneys were a close-knit family and worked together on many social and ministerial concerns. Hannah, Elizabeth's sister, married Sir Thomas Fowell (T.F.) Buxton who succeeded William Wilberforce as the leading voice for abolition in the British Parliament. It was Fowell, as he was known to the family, who introduced the bill that finally brought an end to slavery in Great Britain in 1833. The family also supported Elizabeth's endeavors in prison reform and in opposition to the death penalty. Elizabeth's brothers, Samuel and Joseph John, were avid supporters of her various ministries and contributed financially to her prison reform efforts, as well as joining her on many travels to promote her ideas.

Joseph John Gurney became known as the father of the revivalist movement among Friends. He traveled extensively in the United States as well as in Europe and throughout the British Isles with Elizabeth. His efforts followed on the heels of the Second Great Awakening in the Americas and contributed to another period of spiritual renewal that some have dubbed the "Third Great Awakening." This led to a renewed awareness among

American Friends of the importance of the biblical preaching and teaching which caused many Friends in the south and Midwest to develop a system of pastoral ministry much more akin to that of their neighbors who were of other denominations. Quakers who emphasized the importance of biblical preaching came to be known as "Gurneyites," in recognition of the influence of Joseph John's ministry.

Elizabeth Gurney Fry was truly an exceptional woman. It is hoped that the republication of this brief memoir will awaken present-day readers to her many contributions to our modern society. It is also the desire of this editor that many people, young women in particular, will recognize in Elizabeth an appropriate role model and begin to take leadership in transforming our society into one that is concerned for the welfare of the needy and promotes justice and equality for all persons.

David Goff
December 30, 2006

Chapter One

The Early Years

Elizabeth Gurney Fry was the third daughter of John Gurney, of Earlham, in the county of Norfolk, England. She was born in the year 1781. Her mother, Catherine, died before Elizabeth was twelve years old. Deprived of the care of their beloved mother, the eleven Gurney children were subjected to little restraint. The mind of their indulgent father does not appear to have then yielded to the deep religious convictions that later influenced him. His daughters were allowed to participate in the amusements of a fashionable social life, and also to associate with persons who, while conspicuous for talent and literary research, were skeptical regarding the truths of Christian doctrine. But, while thus exposed to the seductions of vain delights and speculative opinions, a gracious God watched over this interesting family, and, through the renewed spiritual encounters mingled with chastening experiences of sorrow, it pleased their heavenly Father to attract them from the paths of worldly pleasure, and gently lead them in the way of safety and peace.

The first of the sisters who declined the pursuits of frivolous pleasure was Elizabeth. She did not renounce them, however, from any blind subservience to the Christian views of the Society of Friends, of which she was, by birth, a nominal member. A gradually imbibed, but deep-seated conviction of the value of time—of the responsibility of occupying it usefully, and of the powerful influence of example—led her to resist the inclination, so inherent in human nature, to indulge in self-gratification and worldly ease. She was, during her earlier years, remarkable for much originality of thought and quickness of comprehension; was timid, yet very decided in judgment and will; and, even while a child evinced a disposition to promote the well-being, and to soothe the cares and sorrows, of those around her.

Before Elizabeth reached her seventeenth year, she commenced the practice of recording, in the form of a journal, her secret conflicts, and the convictions of religious truth, as they were impressed upon her youthful heart, animating it with love to her Almighty Parent, and to all his intelligent creatures.

In some of her first entries she writes, "I feel by experience how much entering into the world hurts me; worldly company, I think, materially injures; it excites a false stimulus, such as a love of pomp, pride, vanity, jealousy, and ambition; it leads to think about dress and such trifles, and, when out of it, we fly to novels and scandal, or something of that kind, for entertainment. . . . If I have long to live in this world, may I bear misfortunes with fortitude, do what I can to alleviate the sorrows of others, and exert what power I have to increase happiness" (I:18).

"Pride and vanity are too much the incentives to most of the actions of men; they produce a love of admiration, and, in thinking of the opinions of others, we are too apt to forget the monitor within"[3] (I:21).

In her next entry she remarks, "Trifles occupy me far too much, such as dress . . ." (I:22). Again, she describes the effect of frivolous pursuits, "greatly dissipated by hearing the band—idle and relaxed in mind—music has a great effect on me" (I:23). Such were the varied and continuous workings of the opposing influences of nature and grace, in a mind not yet subdued by the power of the Holy Spirit, nor strengthened by a living faith in Christ, who alone can give victory over the world.

Queries for Chapter One

Consider, reflect on, and/or discuss the following queries:

1. How did the loss of Elizabeth's mother influence her early life? Have you experienced the loss of one of your parents or someone else who was very dear to you? In what ways did that loss impact your life?

2. How do you respond to the author's statement, "The mind of their indulgent father does not appear to have then yielded to the deep religious convictions that later influenced him"? Are you able to see growth in your own spiritual life and your convictions about your faith?

3. What experiences, according to the author, led the Gurney children to live "in the way of safety and peace"? Discuss experiences that you have had that have enabled the Spirit to lead you in a similar manner.

4. Why did Elizabeth choose to abandon "the pursuits of frivolous pleasure"? Would you have made the same choice? Do you believe that it would be beneficial for modern day Quakers to come to similar decisions?

5. What is the significance of the journal writing that Elizabeth began as a young woman? Have you read any early Quaker journals? How have they influenced your experience of Quakerism? Is journaling a beneficial exercise for Friends today?

Chapter Two

A Spiritual Awakening

While thus perceiving her own frequent deviations from the path of duty, and conscious that without assistance from on high she could never attain any settled peace of soul, or fulfill the purpose designed by him who had called her into being, it pleased infinite wisdom to direct the steps of one of his gospel messengers—a stranger from a foreign land—to the vicinity of her home. She listened to him (William Savery) as he preached the glad tidings of salvation through a crucified redeemer, and, in a remarkable manner, did the heart-awakening appeal which he was led to utter, find a response in the convictions sealed on her mind by the Holy Spirit. The solemn truths which she heard were but very faintly perceived by her understanding, but she felt that they were blessed realities; and the baptizing power, that accompanied the declaration of them, penetrated the deepest recesses of her soul.[4]

The stability and the soundness of the impressions thus imbibed may be tested by the influence which they exercised over her inclinations and conduct. She was, at this important juncture, taken by her father to London, where she remained several weeks, exposed to a variety of temptations—introduced into the gayest circles of fashionable and polished life, frequenting theatres, the opera, and other places of diversion—all calculated to extinguish the feeble flame of devotion which had been kindled in her bosom; but, having tasted something of the peace and joy that result from yielding to the attractions of the love of God, the enticements of a vain world had lost much of their fascination.

Her journal tells us, "I went to Drury Lane in the evening. I must own that I was extremely disappointed: to be sure the house was grand and dazzling, but I had no other feeling, while there, than that of wishing it over" (I:39). Some days later, she says, "I own I enter into the gay world reluctantly. I do not like plays; I think them so artificial that they are, to me, not interesting, and all seems so—so very far from pure virtue and nature" (I:39).

A few days afterwards she dwells on a different scene: "I went to meeting in the evening. I have not enough eloquence to describe it. William Savery's sermon was, in the first part, very affecting; it was from the Revelations: he explained his text beautifully, and awfully; most awfully I felt it; he next described the sweets of religion and the spirit of prayer: how he did describe it—his prayer was beautiful; I think I felt to pray with him" (I:39). Thus this American visitor, who had been the instrument employed to sow in her heart the seeds of divine truth, was also enabled to water and nurture them. She records the effects of his ministry, and adds, "My idea is that true humility and lowliness of heart is the first grand step towards true religion. I fear and tremble for myself; but I must humbly look to the author of all that is good and great, and, I may say, humbly pray that he will take me as a sheep strayed from his flock, and once more let me enter the fold" (I:40).

Truly, these reflections, penned before she was eighteen years of age, are evidence that she was learning in the school of Christ. In reference to this eventful period of her life she writes, thirty years afterwards:

> Here ended this important and interesting visit to London, where I learned much and had much to digest. I saw and entered various scenes of gaiety, many of our first public places, attended balls, and other places of amusement; I saw many interesting characters in the world, some of them of considerable eminence in that day. It was like the casting die in my life: however, I believe it was in the ordering of providence, and that the lessons then learned are, to this day, valuable to me. I consider one of the important results was the conviction of these things being wrong, from seeing them and feeling their effects: I wholly gave up, on my

own ground, attending all places of amusement: I saw they tended to promote evil; therefore, if I could attend them without being hurt myself, I felt that, in entering them, I lent my aid to promote that, which I was sure (from what I saw) hurt others; led many from the paths of rectitude and chastity, and brought them into much sin. I felt the vanity and folly of what are called the pleasures of this life, of which the tendency is, not to satisfy, but eventually to enervate and injure the heart and mind: those only are real pleasures which are of an innocent nature, and are used as recreations subjected to the Cross of Christ. I was, in my judgment, much confirmed in the infinite importance of religion, as the only real stay, guide, help, and comfort in this life, and the only means of our having a hope of partaking of a better. My understanding was increasingly open to receive its truths, although the glad tidings of the gospel of Christ were little—very little—if at all understood by me: I was like the blind man; I could hardly be said to have attained the state of seeing "men as trees." I obtained in this expedition a valuable knowledge of human character, from the variety I met with—though some were very dangerous associates for so young a person; and the way in which I was protected among them is, in my remembrance, very striking, and leads me to acknowledge that, at this most critical period of my life, the tender mercy of my God was marvelously displayed towards me. Can anyone doubt that it was his Spirit which manifested to me the evil of my own heart, as well as that which I perceived around me; leading me to abhor it, and to hunger and thirst after himself and his righteousness, and that salvation which cometh by Christ? (I:41-2)

Thus were the circumstances of her early life, and the characteristics of her natural mind, rendered subservient to the great work to which she was appointed, and her spirit was shaped into a vessel made holy and useful for the master's use.

Early in life, Elizabeth imbibed, as she says, "very skeptical or deistical principles" but, under the converting influence of divine grace, the Bible became, to her humbled spirit, inexpressibly precious, and the truths of the glorious gospel of Christ were gradually impressed upon her mind (I:47). While not yet eighteen she speaks of her heart being filled with "benevolence and affection," going every day to see a servant living near her home, who was sinking in a decline (I:48). She reads to him the Bible, seeks to comfort him, and supplies his personal necessities. She endeavors watchfully to regulate her conduct by Christian rules: "First; never lose any time—always be in the habit of being employed. Second; never err in the least in truth. Third; never say an ill thing of a person when I can say a good thing: not only speak charitably but feel so. Fourth; never be irritable or unkind to anyone. Fifth; never indulge myself in luxuries that are not necessary. Sixth; do all things with consideration; and when my path to act right is most difficult, feel confidence in that power that alone is able to assist me" (I:49).

The sphere of active duty on which, through the influence of the Savior's love, this young person was gradually induced to enter now became enlarged, and she devoted the evening of each recurring First-day[5] of the week, to the instruction of some of her neighbors, reading to them "the New Testament, and religious books for an hour" (I:51). She also took great delight in forming and superintending a school, on her father's premises, for the poor children of Earlham and the adjoining parishes; and as benevolence became a marked and settled feature of her character, it expelled from her heart the love of pleasure and self-indulgence.

True religion produced its genuine fruits—she could no longer enjoy any recreation that tended to obscure the sense of an ever-present and omnipotent judge, or to draw her from that "fear of the Lord" which "is a fountain of life, preserving from the snares of death . . . How little," she remarks, "is the mind capable of really feeling that we are all in the presence of God, who overlooks every action: should we not tremble when we think of it? Virtue alone can make this thought a happy one" (I:52).

In the summer of 1798, she accompanied her father and sisters on a tour to the west of England and through Wales. While at Plymouth, an officer of the marines invited the party "to hear a very famous marine band." Elizabeth declined to accept his kindness, because she considered it "wrong even to give countenance to a thing that inflames men's minds to destroy each other . . . It is," she says, "truly giving encouragement as far as lies in my power, to what I most highly disapprove, therefore I think I am right to stay at home." On the same day, they went on board a man-of-war. Elizabeth writes, "It was a fine but melancholy sight. I may gain some information by it, but it is not what I quite approve of, the same as the band. My heart feels most anxious, this night, that I may go right, for straight and narrow is the path that leadeth to eternal life, and broad is the way that leadeth to destruction. I feel much satisfaction attending my not going to the review—as soon as I determined to give it up inclination vanished, and now would lead me to stay at home" (I:56).

Some deep emotions, of a character entirely opposed to those which must be excited by dissipating or worldly pleasures, became strongly impressed upon the heart of this youthful traveler; she saw, she remarks, "a sad number of poor sailors and women; I longed to do them good, to try to make them sensible of the evil state they appear to be in" (I:57). The Christian solicitude which thus dwelt on her spirit, originating in the love of God, was of no transient nature. It remained fixed, as in the depths of her spiritual being, during twenty-seven years, until, in 1825, an opportunity presented itself for the outpouring of this hidden spring of gospel interest, by a religious meeting at Devonport, at which more than fifteen hundred (mostly of the lowest class) were addressed by her in a powerfully attractive invitation to repent and turn to God, and do works meet for repentance. In the near prospect of that meeting, her heart, she says, "was ready to fail, fears got hold of me, and almost had dominion over me. I may, I think, say it was, before it ended, a glorious time, much solemnity prevailed amongst us; the power of the great and good Spirit appearing to reign over all. I cannot help humbly trusting that the fruit will remain" (I:476).

But we recur to the journey—the most interesting feature of it was, to the mind of Elizabeth, a visit to Colebrook Dale, where she became associated with some relatives and friends who were conspicuous for piety and benevolence. Several of them were excellent ministers of the gospel. At the close of a pleasant evening, spent in company with her father and sisters, and some members of the families of the Colebrook Dale Friends, all the party became sensible of the presence and love of the heavenly Father, attracting them to that true worship which consists in a deep prostration of the soul and all its faculties in adoration of the Most High; and which, however little it may be comprehended by too many professing Christians, is, assuredly, no cunningly devised fable. Describing the occasion, Elizabeth says, "My heart began to feel itself silenced before God, and without looking at others I found myself under the shadow of his wing, and I soon discovered that the rest were in the same state; my mind felt clothed with light as with a garment" (I:62).

Elizabeth returned from this excursion with a conviction that the line of duty, designed for her by infinite wisdom, was clearly marked as that which would lead her to adopt the habits and language of Friends. Yielding to this impression, she was enabled to enter on a path that eventually led to results that, in their importance and beneficial influence on the human family, could never have been contemplated by the aid of mere human foresight.

On being again settled at home, she resumed her usual habits of visiting and relieving the poor, especially extending help to the sick, reading the Bible to them, and teaching their children. Her school numbered more than seventy pupils. She taught them without assistance, the means of instruction being derived from the stores of knowledge which she had herself obtained by study and reflection: for books suited to their comprehension, or pictorial representations, were not then in use.

Being thus committed to the fulfillment of important duties, she became increasingly capable of rightly estimating the relative value of temporal pursuits. She felt that the amusements, in which she had been accustomed to indulge, involved a waste of that inestimable treasure, time—given to prepare for eternity, and to promote the glory of God: she could no longer derive satisfaction from entering the dance, or from music and singing; yet she exercised a remarkable degree of control over her own feelings, and great caution in assuming habits of self-denial. She writes, "My mind is in an uncomfortable state. I am astonished to find that I have felt a scruple at music—my mind is rather uneasy after I have been spending time in it. These cannot be sensations of my own making, for I have such happiness when I overcome my worldly self, and, when I give way to it, am uneasy" (I:60).

Some selections from her journal may further explain the workings of her mind amid the conflict between nature and grace.

"Tenth month, 17th. I have now two things heavily weighing on my mind—dancing and singing: so sweet and so pretty do they seem: but as surely as I do either, so surely does a dark cloud come over my mind. Can such feelings be my own putting on? They seem to affect my whole frame, mental and bodily. They cannot be from myself. Is it worthwhile to continue in so small a pleasure for so much pain?" (I:68).

"If I could make a rule never to give way to vanity, excitement, or flirting, I do not think I should object to dancing; but it always leads me into some one of these faults; indeed, I never remember dancing without feeling one, if not a little of all the three, and sometimes a great deal" (I:70).

Two months later: "How much my natural heart does love to sing; but, if I give way to the ecstasy that singing sometimes produces on my mind, it carries me far beyond the centre, it increases all the wild passions, and works on enthusiasm. Many say and think that it leads to religion: it may lead to emotions of religion, but true religion appears to me to be in a deeper recess of the heart, where no earthly passion can produce it" (I:74). As she followed the gentle leadings of the Spirit of truth, she became decided in rejecting all that appeared to obstruct her enjoyment of the Savior's love; and she writes, second month, 1799, "I have great reason to believe Almighty God is directing my mind to the haven of peace: at least, I feel that I am guided by a power not my own. I took courage and tried to follow the directions of this voice; I felt enlightened, even happy" (I:73).

Queries for Chapter Two

Consider, reflect on, and/or discuss the following queries:

1. Why do you believe William Savery's preaching had such a powerful impact on Elizabeth? Does that raise any concerns for the young people in our present-day meetings?

2. How did Savery's preaching impact Elizabeth's visit to London? How did Elizabeth respond to London society? What can we learn from her experience to help us deal with our own experiences?

3. How did Elizabeth's view of the Bible and religion develop immediately following her Quaker "baptism"? How does this correspond to your own view of the Bible and religion?

4. What types of ministry did Elizabeth perform early on? How did this help to prepare her for her later ministry experiences? What type of experiential ministry are you involved in or have been involved in?

5. What was the spiritual significance of the journey Elizabeth took with her father and sisters? What do you think of her decision to "adopt the habits and language of Friends"? If you were to decide to "adopt the habits and language of Friends," what would you do differently?

6. What other spiritual "issues" did Elizabeth struggle with upon her return home? What do you think of her conclusions?

Chapter Three

Marriage and Early Days of Ministry

The winter of 1799 brought with it highly important considerations as Elizabeth received a proposal of marriage from Joseph Fry. Her sensitive nature shrunk from so momentous a subject, and, for a time, she seemed unwilling to encounter the responsibility. But, on the renewal of Joseph's request, she gave it her serious attention; and, about eight months afterwards, they were married and became residents of Mildred Court, London. With deep religious feeling, and a devout trust in God, she entered into this solemn engagement. The farewell visits to her indigent neighbors, who had been the recipients of her benevolent care, were mournful to her and to them. Of her students she says, "When all my poor children came, it was rather a melancholy time to me: there were about eighty-six of them: many of them wept; and when they went away, I shed my tears also" (I:94).

In the new sphere in which she was placed, her first desire was that she might faithfully serve her redeemer, and promote in the hearts of those around her the work of his Holy Spirit. Each morning commenced with the daily practice of the family reading together some portion of the Bible. The sorrows of the afflicted and needy excited her usual sympathies. The training of children in habits of industry, and the endeavor to imbue their minds with the fear and love of their creator, continued to claim her ardent attention, and we find her during the first year of her married life visiting the school of Joseph Lancaster. Lancaster's school consisted of a large number of poor, ragged children, crowded into a garret in Southwark. There, struggling with difficulties and embarrassments, the genius of this remarkable youth devised and carried out the system of popular education, now known as that of "the British and Foreign School Society." For the last fifty years, this "Lancasterian System" has been gradually extending Christian education throughout England and in various other regions of the earth. Elizabeth conversed with Lancaster on his school plans; and makes the following judicious reflection, as she refers to the visit, "I felt a wish that the young man might be preserved in humility; but I know, from experience, that it is a hard matter when we have the apparent approbation of many, and particularly of those whom we esteem" (I:105).

In her almsgiving, she was liberal but retiring. In dispensing it, she did not shrink from exertions that involved much sacrifice of personal comfort. She carefully investigated the circumstances of those who applied for relief, and, after a fatiguing "search in one of the most disagreeable parts of the city," she remarks, "I felt quite in my element, serving the poor; and although I was much tired, yet it gave me much pleasure: it is an occupation that my nature is so fond of: I wish not to take merit to myself" (I:117).

Her concern for the physical needs of her fellow-creatures increased as time passed, but there was a spring of divine love in the depths of her soul, which, emanating from the fountain of goodness and blessing, was gradually rising in life and strength, until it surmounted every obstruction, and flowed in streams of heavenly influence, to the comfort and edification of many a fellow Christian.

One of the earliest impressions made on her mind by her religious convictions was that, if faithful to God, she would be called by him to preach the good news of salvation through Christ. Her spirit was, by nature, timid and shrinking, and nothing short of the direction and support of her Almighty Father could prepare her for such a challenging assignment, or guide her safely in the performance of it.

Perhaps, some readers of this book may be inclined to refuse assent to the principle, always recognized by the Society of Friends that, through the operation of the Holy Spirit in the church of Christ, the gift of the ministry is dispensed, without distinction of sex, to individuals called of God to this sacred vocation.[6]

Elizabeth was no stranger to the conflict between a fervent desire to yield, in childlike submission, to the divine will, and the fear lest, in admitting a belief that this most weighty and important service was appointed for her by her Lord, she might be subject to a delusion. For more than eleven years she waited before the prospect which was presented to her mind in youth became mature and realized, and she felt strengthened to follow in the footsteps of holy women who exercised the gift of prophecy, not only under the Mosaic dispensation, but also in the first and purest age of Christianity.

Here let the serious reader, who, while accepting the scriptural record respecting Anna in the temple, and the "four daughters" of Philip "who did prophesy" (Acts 21:9), may nevertheless be disposed to doubt the continuation of this gift to the female sex in the church, meditate on the declaration of the apostle Peter. On the day of Pentecost, he stated that the prediction of the prophet Joel (Joel 2:28) was then fulfilled; "and it shall come to pass in the last days, saith God, I will pour out my Spirit upon all flesh: and your sons and your daughters shall prophesy, and your young men shall see visions, and your old men shall dream dreams, and on my servants and on my handmaidens I will pour out in those days of my Spirit, and they shall prophesy" (Acts 2:17). He also said that this outpouring of the Spirit, and this prophesying both of servants and handmaidens, was not designed to be a merely temporary blessing to the followers of Christ, which is evident from the apostle's added declaration, "The promise is unto you, and to your children, and to all that are afar off, even as many as the Lord our God shall call" (Acts 2:39).

But there is yet another test, which may surely be admitted as affording a conclusive testimony that the mission of this devoted woman was fulfilled in obedience to the manifested will of God. The Lord Jesus has instructed us that "Every tree is known by its fruit" (Matt. 12:33; Luke 6:44). How strikingly were the genuine fruits of the Holy Spirit manifested in the life and conduct of Elizabeth Gurney Fry, and in what varied abundance were her ministerial labors demonstrated to be effective, in planting the seed of Christ's kingdom in many hearts! It was through following, in simple faith, the guidance of her Lord's Spirit, that she became so influenced by his love and power, as to be qualified for the remarkable life of service into which she was led. Subjected to his divine instructions, she was made aware that no finite mind could adequately conceive the unutterable value of an immortal soul, destined to exist in happiness or misery throughout eternity. Her heart overflowed with the boundless love and compassion of Christ so that she willingly resigned every enjoyment, and directed all of her energies, to the purpose of rescuing her fellow mortals from the deadly grasp of Satan, and attracting them to Christ, who alone can deliver from his power.

It was at Norwich, in the year 1809, beside the grave of her beloved father, that, bowed under the mighty hand of God, and brought into a state of deep inward as well as external stillness, her spirit was so filled with a sense of the Savior's presence and love, that she felt constrained to offer, in prayer and praise, a public confession of his goodness and mercy. In recording the circumstances of this solemn day, she says, "a quiet, calm, and invigorated state, mental and bodily, was my portion afterwards" (I:146).

Fervent was her daily prayer for almighty aid and guidance, and her record of the exercises of her devoted spirit indicate that her petitions arose as continual incense. "O Lord," she writes, "I pray thee, preserve thy poor handmaid in the hour of temptation, and enable me to follow thee in the way of thy requirings, even if they lead me into suffering and unto death" (I:153). "I may, in a measure, adapt the language, 'my soul doth magnify the Lord, and my spirit hath rejoiced in God my Savior,' when I feel as I do today—I fear for myself, lest even this great mercy should prove a temptation, and lead me to come before I am called, or enter on service I am not prepared for: but in all these things I have but one place of safety to take refuge in. Be pleased, then, Oh Lord! Thou who knowest my heart and all its temptations, be pleased to preserve me, and enable me to do thy will, in strength and in weakness, when it leads into the hardest crosses, as well as in the way of rejoicing" (I:157).

Elizabeth's services in the ministry were attended with a power and fervent inspiration that humbled and brought to repentance the hearts of her listeners. Her fellow members could, with solemn thankfulness, recognize the gift which they believed to be bestowed on her, by the holy head of the church, for the edification of the body in love. But it was not only by those believers with whom she was most closely associated that the clear stamp of Christian unity was placed on her gospel labors. Many persons of learning and piety manifested their approval, and testified to the powerful efficacy of her ministrations.

On the day when the Bible Society was established at Norwich in 1811, a large company dined at Earlham Hall; Elizabeth was then on a visit there, and at the table she was surrounded by six clergymen of the Established Church, three dissenting ministers, besides some of the Society of Friends. In detailing the circumstances of the day, she says, "a very little before the cloth was removed, such a power came over me of love, I believe I may say life, that I thought I must ask for silence, and then supplicate the Father of mercies for his blessing, both of the fatness of the earth, and of the dew of heaven, upon those who thus desired to promote his cause, by spreading the knowledge of the Holy Scriptures" (I:173). She knelt and offered prayer. "It was," she says, "like having our High Priest amongst us; independently of this power his poor instruments are nothing, but with this power how much is affected! I understood many were in tears, I believe all were bowed down spiritually." Soon after Elizabeth had taken her seat, a Baptist minister said, "This is an act of worship." A clergyman added, "We want no wine, for there is that amongst us that does instead." The excellent and devoted C. F. Steinkoff then expressed his unity, saying that he felt the Spirit of prayer, although, being a foreigner, he could not understand all the words in which it had been uttered. Another clergyman made some weighty remarks on the manner in which the Almighty visited his people; that neither sex, nor anything else, stood in the way of his grace (I:173-4).

Joseph Hughes, one of the secretaries of the Bible Society, gave, in a letter, an interesting description of this occasion, in which he remarks, "after the dinner on the day of the Meeting, the pause encouraged by the Society of Friends was succeeded by a devout address to the deity by a female minister, Elizabeth Fry, whose manner was impressive, and whose words were so appropriate, that none present can ever forget the incident, or ever advert to it without emotions, alike powerful and pleasing. The first emotion was surprise; the second, awe; the third, pious fervor. As soon as we were readjusted at the table, I thought it might be serviceable to offer a remark that proved the coincidence of my heart with the devotional exercise in which we had been engaged; this had the desired effect: Mr. Owen and others suggested accordant sentiments, and we seemed generally to feel like the disciples, whose hearts burned within them as they walked to Emmaus" (I:175).

After being again settled at home, Elizabeth enters in her journal the fervent petitions of her soul, as follows: "May the state of my heart be such, that I may with truth say, Here am I, Lord! do with me what thou wilt, only make me what thou wouldst have me to be. . . . Grant me, O Lord! wisdom and strength to proclaim thy power and thy praise; that, if made use of at all, others, as well as myself, may be drawn nearer to thee, and wholly give thee praise; never taking, or giving, that glory to the creature, which belongs alone to the creator" (I:179).

In allusion to some extended religious engagements, she says, in a letter to a friend, "Having been made instrumental to warn and encourage others, may I not become a cast-away myself—is it not enough to feel a power, better than ourselves, influencing and strengthening us to do the work that, we humbly trust, is the Lord's? For what honor, favor, or blessing is so great as being engaged in the service of him whom we love, in whatever way it be, whether performing one duty or another, and having a little evidence granted us that we are doing his will, or endeavoring to do it? I peculiarly feel, in ministerial duties, that I have no part, because the whole appears a gift—the willing heart, the power, and everything attending it; the poor creature has only to remain passive" (I:184).

Many domestic and related concerns, especially a frequent attendance on the sick and afflicted, called forth the energies of this dedicated Christian. The fervent heavenly love that energized her spirit imparted the ability to console, as well as to instruct, those who were brought low under the chastening hand of the Lord. It especially attracted her to the abject and the wretched. Within half a mile of her country residence at Plashet, there were many of the poorest and most neglected class; a considerable number of them the lowest description of Irish; she often visited them and investigated their necessities, which she relieved with judicious care; supplying clothing and medicines, and, in the winter season, an abundant provision of excellent soup, which furnished a frequent and nutritious meal to hundreds of poor persons. Her unfailing concern for the right training of children motivated her to promote the establishment of a school for girls. It was organized on the Lancasterian system, and soon numbered upwards of seventy. She was a strong advocate of vaccination and, having been instructed by an eminent physician, she was skillful in performing the operation. By her inoculation of the children of her indigent neighbors, smallpox was scarcely ever known in the surrounding villages.

In a lane near Plashet there was annually an encampment of Gypsies, who were attracted there by a fair. Elizabeth assisted them from year-to-year with clothing for their children, frequently with medicines, and with Bibles. At the same time she earnestly exhorted them to forsake sin and to seek the redemption which is in Christ.

Thus varied were the claims upon her sympathy and exertions, as she sought to alleviate the wants and sufferings of those around her. She was not, herself, exempt from many deep trials, and some heavy sorrows, in connection with her own interesting household. She had a large family of young children, to whom she was a most tender and devoted mother. One of these precious treasures—a lovely and precocious little girl—was taken from her affectionate parents before she reached her fifth year. Elizabeth also had to mingle in scenes of great suffering at Earlham, from the decease, first of a sister-in-law, and then of the widowed brother. While she acutely shared in the sense of bereavement, she was enabled to minister consolation to the beloved circle with whom she mourned. In pathetic, yet devout expression, she thus describes her emotions, "Although it pleases my heavenly Father thus to chastise me, yet I am permitted to feel that he doth love those whom he chasteneth: I feel his love very near" (I:236).

Queries for Chapter Three

Consider, reflect on, and/or discuss the following queries:

1. Reflect on Elizabeth's reaction(s) to the proposal of marriage from Joseph Fry. What does this suggest to us today about dealing with important decisions?

2. What was Elizabeth's first concern in her new role as a married woman? How does this compare to the concerns of modern women?

3. What type of ministry activities did Elizabeth enter into as a newly married woman? In what direction did her increasing maturity move her? Have you experienced a major life change that resulted in a change in your ministry activities?

4. What arguments are made by the author in favor of women in a preaching ministry? Do you agree or disagree with those arguments? Are there other arguments that you might add to these? When you listen to a person who is preaching, do you find the person's gender to be an obstacle?

5. What event sparked the beginning of Elizabeth's vocal ministry? Why?

6. What event is given in the text to corroborate the public recognition of Elizabeth's gift of spoken ministry? Have you ever had an opportunity to address a meeting in spoken ministry?

7. What other ministries did Elizabeth participate in as recorded in this chapter? What types of ministries are you involved in? Are you exercising the gifts for ministry with which God has endowed you?

Chapter Four

Ministering to those in Prison

For a considerable time Elizabeth was concerned on behalf of the most miserable and degraded portion of the community—the inmates of prisons. On a very moving occasion (one which was then almost continually occurring)—the execution of several convicts—four members of the Society of Friends obtained admittance to the great metropolitan jail of Newgate. There they had an opportunity of expressing their deep concern on behalf of these poor criminals who were about to be hurried into the presence of an omniscient judge. The benevolent visitors had permission also to pass into that portion of the building in which the women were confined. The report of these Friends, particularly that of the late William Forster, induced Elizabeth to inspect the conditions in the female department of the prison. It was an intensely cold season, and the sufferings of the wretched women were, from their being destitute of sufficient clothing, so great as to demand immediate efforts to relieve them.

At that time all the female prisoners in Newgate were crowded together into two wards and two cells. These four rooms contained nearly three hundred women, with their numerous children. They consisted of the tried and untried, those guilty of misdemeanors and felons, without any classification, without employment, and with no other superintendence than that of a man and his son who had the charge of them by night and by day. In the same rooms did these poor creatures live, cook, and wash, sleeping without bedding on the floor, the boards of which inclined upwards against the wall to supply the want of a pillow. Thus, covered with a few tattered garments, filthy in the extreme, affording scarcely any protection from the inclemency of the weather, were these miserable women first visited by Elizabeth. She was accompanied by Anna Buxton.

The scene on which they were about to enter was one of the wildest disorder. Drunkenness prevailed to a fearful extent: for the prisoners were visited by many of their former degraded associates, who responded to their clamorous begging by giving them money, with which they purchased beer and spirits from a regular tap in the prison. Swearing, gambling, and fighting filled up every hour of the day. Even the governor was reluctant to enter this portion of the building. He advised the two female Friends to leave their watches and purses under his care, fearing they would be snatched from them, but this kind suggestion was not acted upon. Faith and love divested them of all fear of danger, and, without the protection of man, they ventured among this disorganized multitude. The sorrowful and neglected condition of both women and children deeply affected their hearts, and Elizabeth used much exertion to prepare and supply suitable clothing for the destitute.

On the occasion of their third visit, she makes the following entry in her journal: "Yesterday we were some hours at Newgate with the poor female felons, attending to their outward necessities. We had been twice previously. Before we went away, dear Anna Buxton uttered a few words in supplication; and, very unexpectedly to myself, I did also. I heard weeping, and I thought they appeared much tendered: a very solemn quiet was observed: it was a striking scene; the poor people on their knees around in their deplorable condition" (I:201).

The efforts which Elizabeth had made to alleviate the miseries of these wretched beings could not escape notice—they elicited great approval, particularly from many of her most esteemed friends; and, as it was manifested by expressions of unity, it raised in her heart a fervent prayer that her humility and dependence on her Lord be preserved. She writes, under date of Second month, 15th, 1814, "My fear for myself, the last few days, is, lest I should be exalted by the evident unity of my dear friends whom I greatly value; and also my natural health and spirits being good; and being engaged in some laudable pursuits; more particularly seeing after the prisoners in Newgate. Oh, how deeply, how very deeply, I fear the temptation of ever being exalted, or self-conceited! I cannot preserve myself from this temptation, any more than being unduly cast down, or crushed by others. Be pleased; O Lord! to preserve me: for the deep inward prayer of my heart is; that I may ever walk humbly before thee; and also before all mankind. Let me never, in any way, take that glory to myself which belongs alone unto thee, if, in thy mercy, thou shouldst ever enable one so unworthy either to do good" (I:200).

A considerable time elapsed before Elizabeth again visited the Newgate prison. During the interval, many important events occurred, and she was variously exercised in the school of affliction. She was permitted to endure much bodily indisposition, her husband was subjected to considerable loss of property, and death removed from her some tenderly beloved friends. Yet, she was frequently constrained, through the influence of the Lord's Spirit, to devote herself to his service in the ministry of the word. Her labors were remarkably blessed to the arousing of the indifferent, the comforting of the mourners, and the strengthening of many who were weak in the ranks of her fellow disciples.

The destitute and the ignorant of every class were, as their necessities became known to her, still the objects of her care. But no occupations, conflicts, or sufferings, could efface from her heart the impression which it had received on her visits to Newgate. Deep and solemn was her interest on behalf of the degraded inmates of that receptacle of vice and misery. A conviction became gradually impressed on her spirit that she was called by him, by whom she had been enabled to dedicate every talent committed to her trust, to labor as he might see fit to open the way before her, for the moral reformation of those who had rendered themselves detestable to the penalties of justice. Most especially did she feel a persuasion that it was the design of the merciful redeemer, that she should yield herself his willing instrument in seeking to awaken perishing sinners, slumbering on the verge of endless perdition, and to invite them to come unto him who alone could bring them "from darkness to light, and from the power of Satan unto God" (Acts 26:18).

Nothing short of the operation of divine love could have produced, in the mind of this refined and delicate woman, a willingness to forego domestic comfort, congenial association, and personal ease, and even to risk her own reputation, and to enter upon a line of service most arduous and painful, from which her nature recoiled with dread. But animated by the full belief that the sacrifice was required by her Lord, and humbly depending on his help and strength, her faith surmounted every obstacle; and she entered on the peculiar sphere of duty, which, through the remainder of her remarkable life, engaged so large a share of her benevolent efforts. She ventured again amongst the female prisoners in Newgate: she found them sunk into a condition of the utmost depravity; yet so wonderfully did the sense of her divine master's presence and power sustain her spirit, that she requested to be left alone with them.

She remained with them for some hours. Her dignified deportment and her gentle accents of love and kindness, restrained their ferocity, and she succeeded at length, in her attempts to gain their quiet attention, while she read to them the parable of the Lord of the vineyard; afterwards addressing them on the eleventh hour, and on Christ having come to save sinners, even those who might have passed the greater portion of their lives in estrangement from him. She particularly noticed the children, pining for want of proper food, air, and exercise, and almost without clothing. She endeavored to impress on the mothers the grievous circumstances in which their misconduct had involved their helpless offspring, and when the hearts of these wretched women were, in some measure, softened, she proposed to them the establishment of a school, to which they readily assented.

She desired them to consider the plan, leaving them to select a governess from among themselves. On the following day she again visited them, being then accompanied by her friend Mary Sanderson, who thus described the scene: "The railing was crowded with half-naked women, struggling together for the front situations with the most boisterous violence, and begging with the utmost vociferation. . . . [She] felt as if she were going into a den of wild beasts—quite shuddering when the door was closed, and she was locked in with such a herd of novel and desperate companions" (I:257). These benevolent visitors were, however, able to organize the projected school, and the prisoners had selected a young woman to act as mistress of it, who proved peculiarly suited to the task, and who became one of the first fruits of the Christian labor in the prison, giving evidence of a real conversion. She received a free pardon, but she was soon affected by pulmonary disease. After enduring her illness with much patience and obtaining, as there was good ground to believe, peace and reconciliation with God, through a gracious redeemer, she died in the hope of a blessed immortality. But it was not until repeated efforts had been made for the improvement of these wretched women, that their brutal propensities became permanently restrained.

On a subsequent occasion, another faithful coadjutor in the work, Elizabeth Pryor, found them, as she says, "seated about the yard, with ferocious countenances. . . . From the prison-door one issued [(probably a felon just then brought to the jail)] yelling like a wild beast: she rushed round the area, with her arms extended, tearing everything of the nature of a cap from the heads of the other women." But this very woman was through the grace and mercy of God, humanized under the instruction of these Christian visitors. She became "a well-conducted person," and married respectably (I:257).

Elizabeth's attentiveness to affect a reform in the habits of these miserable outcasts was cordially approved by the sheriffs of London, the governor and chaplain of Newgate, and by other influential persons. Yet, with scarcely any exception, the attempt to reduce to order such an unruly and vicious assemblage soon became viewed as the result of a merely visionary scheme, and discouragements were presented on every hand. At a subsequent period, she was required to give evidence before the House of Commons, respecting the condition in which she had found the female department of the prison, and of her success in endeavoring to remedy the evils which abounded there. She stated that it was in their daily visits to the school that they were "witnesses of the dreadful proceedings that went forward, the begging, swearing, gaming, fighting, singing, dancing, dressing up in men's clothes; scenes too bad to be described, so that we did not think it suitable to admit young persons with us" (I:257).

Elizabeth, and the heroic little band that joined her in the engagement, became convinced that some good at least might be affected by proper regulations. Their kindness towards the prisoners had won their respect, and their own minds were inspired with hope and confidence. With remarkable wisdom Elizabeth made arrangements for a code of laws to be observed by the prisoners. She formed a committee, consisting of the wife of a clergyman and eleven members of the Society of Friends, who, in 1817, were regularly organized as "An Association for the Improvement of the Female Prisoners in Newgate." They stated their purpose "to provide for the clothing, the instruction, and the employment of the women; to introduce them to a knowledge of the Holy Scriptures; and to form in them, as much as possible, those habits of order, sobriety, and industry, which may render them docile and peaceable while in prison, and respectable when they leave it" (I:262).

The concurrence of the city magistrates was obtained, but much doubt was expressed as to how far the women would submit to the requisite restraints and regulations. To ascertain their dispositions on this all-important question, the sheriffs met the members of the Association at the prison. The women were assembled, and in the presence of the sheriffs, the governor, and the ordinary, they were asked by Elizabeth whether they were willing to abide by the rules which were so indispensable for the accomplishment of the object so much desired by all. The women fully and unanimously assured her of their determination to obey them strictly. The sheriffs addressed them on the importance of observing these rules.

Having thus far succeeded, the next business was to provide employment for the prisoners, and a suitable apartment for their industrial occupation. The latter object was immediately attended to by the sheriffs, who sent carpenters to prepare a work room, and the partners of a respectable house in London arranged to supply articles for the prisoners' manufacture. A few days afterwards, the committee met in the large apartment which had been fitted up. All the women being assembled, Elizabeth addressed them: "She began by describing to them the comforts to be derived from industry and sobriety, and contrasted the happiness and peace of those who are dedicated to a course of virtue and religion, with the sad experience of their former life and its consequences; and, alluding to their awful guilt in the sight of God, appealed to themselves whether its wages, even here, were not utter misery and ruin. She then dwelt upon the motives which had brought her and her associates into Newgate: they had left their homes and their families to mingle amongst those from whom all others fled, animated by an ardent and affectionate desire to rescue their fellow-creatures from evil" (I:265).

She then told them that it was "not intended that the visitors should command and the prisoners obey, but it was to be understood that all were to act in concert; that not a rule should be made, or a monitor appointed, without their full and unanimous concurrence; that, for this purpose, each of the rules should be read and put to the vote: and she invited those who might feel any disinclination to any particular, freely to state their opinions" (I:290).

The rules were then read; and, as each was proposed, every hand was held up in token of approbation. With the same formalities each of the monitors was proposed, and all were unanimously approved. When this business was concluded, one of the visitors read aloud the twenty-first chapter of Matthew—the parable of the barren fig tree being applicable to the state of the audience. After a period of silence, the monitors, with their respective classes withdrew to their wards in the most orderly manner.

Within a few days from this most interesting occasion, the lord mayor, the sheriffs, and several of the aldermen attended the morning reading of the Bible. They requested that no alteration in the usual practice should take place. The prisoners were assembled. One of the committee read a chapter, then, after a pause of silence, the women proceeded to their various avocations. An eye-witness who described the scene added, "their attention during the time of reading, their orderly and sober deportment, their decent dress, the absence of everything like tumult, noise, or contention, the obedience and respect shown by them, and the cheerfulness visible in their countenances and manners, conspired to excite the astonishment and admiration of their visitors. Many of these knew Newgate, had visited it a few months before, and had not forgotten the painful impressions made by a scene exhibiting, perhaps, the very utmost limits of misery and guilt" (I:267).

Encouraged by many concurring circumstances, the newly formed Ladies' Committee now introduced a matron into Newgate. The prisoners were divided into classes and placed under her superintendence, but some of the committee, who had been in the regular practice of spending the whole of each day in the oversight and instruction of these poor outcasts, continued to pass some hours daily in this important field of labor. The surveillance of the "man and his son," who had before had the entire charge of the women, was dispensed with, and the corporation of London shared with the committee the expenses incurred by the substitution of female attendants. The following description of the contrast between the former circumstances of the prisoners and those which now marked their condition may be introduced. It was penned by a gentleman of respectability:

> I went and requested permission to see Mrs. Fry, and was conducted by a turnkey to the entrance of the women's wards. On my approach no loud or dissonant sounds or angry voices indicated that I was about to enter a place which had long had the appellation of "Hell above ground." The courtyard, into which I was admitted, instead of being peopled with beings scarcely human, blaspheming, fighting, tearing each others' hair, or gaming with a filthy pack of cards for the very clothes they wore (which often did not suffice even for decency), presented a scene where stillness and propriety reigned. I was conducted by a decently dressed person, the newly appointed yards woman, to the door of a ward, where, at the head of a long table, sat a lady belonging to the Society of Friends. She was reading aloud to about sixteen women prisoners who were engaged in needlework around it. Each wore a clean-looking blue apron

and bib; with a ticket having a number on it suspended from her neck by a red tape. They all rose on my entrance, curtsied respectfully, and then, at a signal given, resumed their seats and employments. Instead of a scowl, leer, or ill-suppressed laugh, I observed upon their countenances an air of self-respect and gravity, a sort of consciousness of their improved character and the altered position in which they were placed. I afterwards visited the other wards, which were the counterparts of the first. (I:268-9)

But we must recur to the journal of Elizabeth Fry, in order to observe the feelings and motives which influenced her as she entered upon and proceeded with the arduous and weighty engagements which we have briefly detailed. Shortly after her earliest renewed visits to the prison, she writes, "I have been much occupied lately in forming a school in Newgate for the children of the poor prisoners, as well as young criminals, which has brought much peace and satisfaction with it; but my mind has been also deeply affected, in attending a poor woman who was executed this morning. I visited her twice: this has been a time of deep humiliation to me, thus witnessing the consequences of sin. How should we watch and pray that we fall not by little and little become hardened and commit greater sins" (I:252).

To her beloved sister, Rachel Gurney, an excellent and faithful helper who had taken charge of some of her children thus liberating Elizabeth for a wider field of philanthropic exertion, she addressed the following lines, in the spring of 1817: "My heart, and mind, and time, are very much engaged in various ways. Newgate is a principal object, and I think that until I make some attempt at amendment in the plans for the women, I shall not feel easy: but if such efforts should prove unsuccessful, I think that I should then have tried to do my part, and be easy. I have felt, in thy taking care of my dearest girls, that thou art helping me to get on with some of these important objects, that I could not well have attended to if I had had all my dear flock around me" (I:252-3).

Her journal contains some most deeply affecting descriptions of her attendance on the wretched convicts, sentenced to terminate their criminal course at the gallows. There were, she says near the time of the last-mentioned date, a young woman, with six men, and the wife of one of them, whose execution was deferred because she was about to add to her miserable family, already consisting of seven children. These victims of a bloody and cruel code of law were varied in character. Some were obdurate and brutalized, others were educated and philosophical. The husband of the poor woman before alluded to was in a state of maniacal frenzy, and the first-named young woman (condemned for being an accessory to robbing in a dwelling-house),[7] "much hurried, distressed, and tormented in mind. Her hands were cold and covered with something like the perspiration preceding death and in a universal tremor" (I:259). But a few hours before she was launched into eternity, Elizabeth, at the unhappy creature's earnest entreaty, spent some time with her in "the condemned cell," and adds, "After a serious time with her, her troubled soul became calmed. But is it for man thus to take the prerogative of the Almighty into his own hands? Is it not his place rather to reform such, or restrain them from the commission of further evil? At least to afford poor, erring fellow-mortals, an opportunity of proving their repentance by amendment of life?" (I:259).

Scenes, like that on which the reader has now dwelt, and which surely no feeling mind can contemplate without a thrill of horror, were of frequent recurrence. Often was the sensitive heart of this devoted Christian harrowed to its utmost depth, as she visited, on the day or the night before they suffered, the wretched criminals whose lives were forfeited through the penal statutes then enforced. With self-sacrificing love she encountered the most appalling circumstances. She sympathized with the extremes of human misery, ministering with words of solemn warning, or pointing the abased and penitent sinner to that Almighty Redeemer, who "was manifested that he might destroy the works of the devil" (1 John 3:8), and whose power is sufficient to rescue from his grasp, even those who are sunk in the lowest gulf of vice, degradation, and woe. Most deeply impressive were the opportunities when, in the felon's dungeon, her fervent prayers were offered on behalf of those who were doomed to expiate their transgressions, by a violent and ignominious transition from the bar of the fallible mortal judge to the inconceivably awful tribunal of an omniscient and Holy God.

The journal proceeds: "My mind and time have been much taken up with Newgate. I feel encouraged about our school; but I have suffered much about the hanging of the criminals. May I, in this important concern, be enabled to keep my eye singly unto the Lord, that what I do may be done heartily unto him, and not, in any degree, unto man. May I be preserved humble, faithful, and persevering in it, as far as it is right to persevere. And, if consistent with the divine will, may the blessing of the Most High attend it; that it may be made instrumental in drawing some out of evil, and leading and establishing them in the way everlasting, where they may find rest and peace" (I:259).

A month later we read the following entry: "I have found, in my late attention to Newgate, a peace and prosperity in the undertaking that I seldom, if ever, remember to have done before. A way has very remarkably been opened for us, beyond all expectation, to bring into order the poor prisoners. Those who are in power are very willing to help us: in short, the time appears come to work amongst them. Already, from being like wild beasts, they appear harmless and kind. I am ready to say, in the fullness of my heart, surely it is the Lord's doing, and marvelous in our eyes; so many are the providential openings of various kinds. Oh! if good should result, may the praise and glory of the whole be entirely given where it is due by us, and by all, in deep humiliation and prostration of spirit" (I:261).

In a letter to her two eldest daughters, who, for nearly a year, had been the guests of their uncle, Daniel Gurney, at Runcton, under the care of their aunt, Rachel Gurney, Elizabeth writes, "Sixth month, 11th, 1817. Remember, my dear children, that if you wish to be real helpers to me and to your dear father, you must take heed to yourselves, and seek to keep your eye single to him, who alone can enable you to do your duty towards yourselves, or towards us. For I am more and more convinced that, unless what we do is done heartily unto the Lord, it profiteth little, and availeth nothing. I cannot tell you, for I have not language to express it, the longing that I have that you, my sweet, dear children may go on in the right way. How far before all other things do I ask it for you, that, while here, you may be guided by his counsel, and afterwards received into glory" (I:280).

On the twentieth she welcomed her boys from school and her girls from Runcton, and writes, "To be once more surrounded by our sweet flock is pleasant, and appears cause for much thankfulness. May a blessing attend us amongst them, so that, in word and in deed, we may preach Christ: and, O gracious Lord! be pleased so to prosper our labors that they may all grow in grace, and in the knowledge of thee" (I:280). "Seventh month, 21st. I seem kept almost always, by night and by day, going again and again to the mercy-seat. I can hardly express what I have felt at times: groanings unutterable for my children, on their getting out of childhood, in their many temptations" (I:281).

Queries for Chapter Four

Consider, reflect on, and/or discuss the following queries:

1. What was the initial motivation that sparked Elizabeth's interest in and concern for the female prisoners at Newgate? What were the conditions under which the women at Newgate were living? Are you aware of the conditions of the needy in your own community?

2. How did the prisoners respond to Elizabeth and the others who came to minister to them? How have you been received when you have tried to minister to others?

3. What did Elizabeth and her associates do for the children of the incarcerated women? Are there children in your community who you can help?

4. How did Elizabeth organize her efforts? What are some of the barriers she faced in establishing this ministry? Have you ever faced barriers when beginning a new ministry?

5. What indications of Quaker thought and practice may be seen in the methods used by Elizabeth and her associates? Does your Meeting reflect Quaker thought and practice in your methods of ministry?

Chapter Five

Enlarging the Scope of Prison Ministry

Elizabeth had no desire for her labors, or those of her benevolent associates in the prison cause, to become subjects of public notoriety. But, during the autumn of 1817, a gentleman who had witnessed the marvelous reformation effected in many who had been amongst the most vicious of the community published a description of the efforts which had been made there, and the results were produced in some of the leading journals. This circumstance, though painful to Elizabeth's humble spirit, was permitted for the welfare of many as it captured public attention as to the necessity of a general improvement in prison discipline. In reference to it she says, "My having been brought publicly forward in the newspapers, respecting what I have been instrumental in doing at Newgate, has brought some anxiety with it: in the first place, as far as I am concerned, that it may neither raise me too high, nor sink me too low, that having what may appear my good works thus published may never lead me, or others, to give either the praise or glory where it is not due. May I in this, and in all other things, experience preservation; for indeed, I cannot keep myself; may I be kept humble, watchful, faithful, and persevering" (I:281-2).

"Oh! the watchfulness required, not to bow to man, not to seek to gratify self-love, but rather, in humility and godly fear, to abide under the humiliation of the cross. Lord, be pleased so to help and strengthen me in this, that, for thine own cause's sake, for my own soul's sake, and for the sake of my beloved family, I may, in no way, be a cause of reproach; but, in my life, conduct, and conversation: may I glorify thy great and ever excellent name" (I:283).

"Twelfth month, 17th. A remarkable blessing still appears to accompany my prison concerns, perhaps the greatest apparent blessing on my deeds that ever attended me. How have the spirits, both of those in power and the poor, afflicted prisoners, appeared to be subjected! Most assuredly the power and the glory is alone due to the author and finisher of every good work. Things in this way thus prosper beyond my most sanguine expectations; but there are also deep humiliations for me" (I:285).

Important duties, connected with the religious Society of which Elizabeth was a highly esteemed member, claimed no inconsiderable portion of her time. Her concern for the spiritual welfare of her friends was frequently manifested, by her Christian exhortations and by her fervent prayers that her fellow-believers might, through the powerful visitations of the Holy Spirit, be favored to grow in grace, and in the knowledge of our Lord and Savior Jesus Christ. The state of the prison having become so effectually improved, her attention to its concerns could be safely relaxed, and the labor more satisfactorily shared by others. She continued, however, to visit it several times during each week.

Many letters were addressed to her by persons of influence: magistrates anxious to institute a process of reform in prisons under their control, and benevolent individuals of both sexes wishing to aid in the work. All wrote seeking for her counsel and assistance, thus requiring her to spend many hours in replying to these communications. Some of the most distinguished and influential persons in the kingdom desired to witness the reformed condition of Newgate, and Elizabeth was consequently required to accompany them. Not a few of these became conspicuously enlisted in the cause of philanthropy, devoting their energies to the amelioration of prison discipline, and to the repeal of the most sanguinary enactments of the penal code. Elizabeth received efficient and persevering aid from the late Sir T. F. Buxton. He had married her beloved sister, Hannah Gurney, and they were united to her, not only in the bonds of family and tender affection, but also by the powerfully motivating principle of Christian philanthropy.

The altered arrangements of the prison entailed heavy financial expenses, demanding resources which could not prudently be supplied, without an appeal to the generosity of benevolent friends. This appeal was most cordially responded to by some wealthy individuals, particularly by several of the near connections of Elizabeth. Her brothers, Samuel and Joseph John Gurney, were especially, and at all times, her unfailing helpers. They conscientiously approved her religious course and her efforts for the public good, and they contributed largely towards the promotion of them. Not a year passed by during the period allotted her for service on earth in which these noble-hearted Christians did not place at her disposal a large amount from the funds entrusted to their stewardship.

When the regulations at Newgate had become firmly established, a necessity no longer existed for such indefatigable labor as had, for a considerable time, been indispensable. As several of the associated committee now shared between them the duty of visiting and instructing the prisoners, one of them assembling the women for a Scripture reading daily, Elizabeth's attendance became more limited. On one particular day of each week she, however, devoted the forenoon to this important engagement, undertaking herself the public reading of the Bible: an office which she performed with peculiar solemnity and sweetness. The prison was, on the appointed morning, open to such visitors as it appeared suitable to admit, and her readings were attended by a great number of persons, both English and foreign, who were anxious to witness this extraordinary scene of order and reformation.

Elizabeth was deeply imbued with earnest desire for the everlasting well-being of every class among men. None were too exalted in earthly station, none too highly endowed by nature or by science, to share the deep solicitudes of her spirit. Her prayers ascended to the throne of grace, for the outpouring of that heavenly influence which alone could attract them to the fountain of mercy and peace.

But her sympathies were, in an especial manner, directed, in unspeakable yearnings, towards the wretched and debased. Their misery, inseparable from sin and condemnation, stirred up from its depth every spring of tender commiseration which could flow into her bosom. The invitations of the redeemer who "came to call sinners to repentance" (Mark 2:17;

Luke 5:32) were often uttered by her with thrilling "demonstration of the Spirit and of power" (1 Cor. 2:4). Many a heart that had been enslaved by the prince of darkness, and rendered obdurate by yielding itself his willing servant, was softened and bowed in penitence, through that constraining love which communicated its efficacious energy to those ministrations, by which, "in Christ's stead" (2 Cor. 5:20), she besought the wanderer and the prodigal to return unto the Father's house and to become reconciled to God.

The attention of Elizabeth and of the visiting committee was by no means confined to Newgate. The female criminals in the other prisons of the metropolis soon came under their care. The confidence which was reposed in them by successive governments was evinced by the convict ships, in which females were transported to New South Wales, being placed under their especial care and superintendence. This was a most important part of their service, and the success that followed the admirable regulations which they introduced into those vessels, was frequently acknowledged by the colonial authorities. Every poor convict was supplied with a variety of articles, needful to mitigate the sufferings attendant on the passage to the distant colony, and each one furnished with a copy of the Holy Scriptures.

It had been always the practice, on their removal from the prisons to the ships at Deptford, to convey them in open wagons amid assembled crowds, the prisoners and those who surrounded them being alike noisy and riotous, the disorder being maintained on the road, and in the boats. Elizabeth prevailed on the governor to consent to their being taken in hackney coaches. The women were quiet and orderly, and she closed the procession by following them in her own carriage. Instead of the former plan, of herding together the convicts and their children in an inadequate space below the deck of the vessel, they were now, through the excellent arrangements of Elizabeth and her faithful helpers, divided into classes, with a monitor (chosen by themselves) appointed to each. They were also supplied with work, which produced a profit received exclusively by the prisoners. An apartment was prepared for a schoolroom, one of the convicts being voluntarily engaged as mistress, for which service she was paid at the end of the voyage from a sum placed by the committee in the hands of the captain. A religious meeting with the poor women closed their personal communication with their benefactress. Solemnly impressive were these farewell interviews. Many a mournful tear trickled down the cheeks of these desolate outcasts, and their sobs and their exclamations of sorrow followed their excellent friend, till they could see her no more.

The influence which, by the force of kindness alone, Elizabeth maintained over the prisoners can scarcely be conceived. They regarded her with the deepest reverence, mingled with grateful love: one of them said it was "more terrible to be brought up before Mrs. Fry than before the judge" (I:288). On one occasion she was informed that some were still gaming in the prison. She went alone, assembled the women, and told them what she had heard; that she feared it was true; dwelt on the evil effects of the sinful practice, and on the grief which the report had caused her, concluding with remarking that she should consider it a proof of their regard, if they would have the candor and the kindness to bring their cards to her. Soon after she had retired to the ladies room, there was a gentle tap at the door, and in came a trembling girl, who, in a manner that indicated much feeling, expressed her sorrow for having broken the rule of so kind a friend. She handed to Elizabeth her pack of cards; she was soon followed by another, and then by three others, until five packs were received, which Elizabeth burned in their presence; assuring the transgressors that, so far from being remembered against them, she should think of it in another way. A few days afterwards they received presents—the first-named girl was, by her own particular desire, favored with a Bible. She had been a very bad girl, had conducted herself extremely ill on her trial; but she became orderly and amiable, so that she appeared "almost without a flaw," and it was "hoped would become a valuable member of society" (I:293).

At this time, the marquis of Lansdowne moved for an address from the House of Lords to the prince regent, on the state of the prisons in the United Kingdom. He dwelt on "the efforts of that very meritorious individual, Mrs. Fry, who had come like the genius of good into the scene of misery and vice, and had, by her wonderful influence and exertions produced, in a short time, a most extraordinary reform amongst the most abandoned class" (I:321). The speech of the marquis renewed, with still greater intensity, the interest which had already been excited, and admittance into Newgate was sought, with eager curiosity, by persons of almost every class: bishops, clergymen, magistrates, officers, and ladies of rank and influence.

Queries for Chapter Five

Consider, reflect on, and/or discuss the following queries:

1. Despite her personal concerns, what positive results came from the publication of Elizabeth's efforts at prison reform in the media of her day? Reflect on the positive and negative results of media coverage of ministry in the modern world.

2. As Elizabeth's ministry at Newgate became more established, and others began to shoulder more of the daily activities, what was the next step in her work for prison reform? How did this tend to enlarge the scope of her ministry? Are there ways that you can share responsibility and expand the scope of your ministry?

3. What reception did Elizabeth receive from public officials? Do you agree that Quakers should seek to have such an impact on society? Why, or why not?

4. What was the initial source of funding for her desired reforms? How should Quakers today finance their ministries?

5. How did the prisoners respond to Elizabeth's ongoing ministry among them? How do people respond to you when you exercise your gifts of ministry?

6. Would you consider Elizabeth's efforts at prison reform to be a success? Why, or why not?

7. Friends believe that every follower of Christ is a minister. How do you see that expressed and encouraged in your meeting/church?

Chapter Six

A Union of Christian Effort

During the succeeding autumn, Elizabeth, accompanied by her brother, Joseph John Gurney, left the scene of her labors on a tour to the north of England and Scotland. In the course of their journey they attended many meetings of their own religious community, in which they were enabled to preach the unsearchable riches of Christ, to the edification of many. These assemblies were of a mingled character. Wherever they went, the name Elizabeth Fry had already been regarded with veneration, and large numbers desired to obtain a personal knowledge of her. After alluding to the attendance of meetings, and to visits to the members of their own Society, she wrote, "We have inspected many prisons. In our religious services our gracious helper has appeared very near. I have felt, at seasons, as leaving all for my master's sake, and setting out without much of purse or scrip; but how bountifully am I provided for, internally and externally. The great shepherd of the sheep has been near to me in spirit, as strength in my weakness, riches in my poverty, and a present helper in the needful time" (I:325).

After the completion of this journey, the result of their observations on the state of the prisons, lunatic asylums, etc., all which were in a most deplorable condition, were published in a pamphlet entitled "Notes on a Visit to Prisons." This raised an increased and general feeling of sympathy with suffering fellow-creatures imprisoned in these receptacles of vice and misery.

"Notes on a Visit to Prisons" was the means of effecting a most important change in the views of many persons in public office. The dukes of Sussex and Gloucester became earnest advocates for the reform of the penal code. The latter accompanied Elizabeth into one of the cells at Newgate in order to visit a poor young woman condemned to suffer death for a trifling degree of complicity in a case of forgery.

In 1821, Sir James Mackintosh brought forward in Parliament a motion "for mitigating the severity of punishment in certain cases of forgery and the crimes connected therewith." He was nobly supported by the late Sir T. F. Buxton. The arguments of these two enlightened and patriotic men, based on facts and incontrovertible evidence, aroused to conviction many in that assembly. Although a small majority opposed to the bill slowed, for a time, the success of the measure, the sentiment that the termination of human existence belongs to the prerogative of an infallible judge gradually became so far diffused throughout the nation that, not only for cases of forgery but for all other crimes excepting willful murder, the terrible penalty of death was annulled.

Elizabeth's occupations in prisons did not supersede the exercise of charity in the vicinity of her own home. Attention to the neighboring poor, and to the school, now devolved chiefly on her two elder daughters, whom she early trained to habits of benevolence, and they proved, in many respects, her efficient helpers. New claims on her sympathies and her cares were continually presented; and no variety of human suffering, comprehended within the sphere of her mental vision, passed before her unheeded, or if within the reach of her kindly influence, without an effort for its relief.

During the rigorous winter of 1819, the sufferings of homeless wanderers in the streets of London deeply touched the heart of this Christian philanthropist. One case was truly agonizing—that of a little boy who had, in vain, begged at many houses for the few half-pence required to procure him a night's lodging in some passage or cellar. He was, at several public houses, refused admittance unless he could furnish three pence. This he could not obtain and in the morning he was found dead on a doorstep. Through Elizabeth's exertions, an asylum was immediately provided. It was well-warmed; nutritious soup was prepared night and morning with a ration of bread for each one sheltered there; and straw beds were furnished.

The generosity of the public afforded the necessary funds. Many hundreds were every evening admitted to the shelter. Employment of various kinds was supplied, and the females were placed under the care of a ladies committee, with Elizabeth at their head.

The deep interest, which the distress of her fellow-creatures continually impressed upon her heart, did not exclude a Christian solicitude for the spiritual well-being of her friends. Nor did it in any degree lessen the tender affection which she invariably cherished towards her endeared family connections. Her engagements in the ministry were edifying and comforting to her fellow-members, and also to other pious individuals. On returning home from a journey, she made the following striking entry in her journal: "I was carried through the service to my own surprise: I felt so remarkably low, so unworthy, so unfit, and as if I had little or nothing to communicate to them, but I was marvelously helped from meeting to meeting; strength so arose with the occasion that the fear of man was taken from me, and I was enabled to declare gospel truths boldly. This is to me wonderful; it must be the Lord's doing, and is marvelous in our eyes how he strengtheneth them that have no might, and helpeth those that have no power! The peace that I felt after the services, for some days, seemed to flow like a river, covering all my cares and sorrows, so that I might truly say, 'There is (even here) a rest for the people of God' (Heb. 4:9). My skeptical, doubting mind has been convinced of the truth of religion, not by the hearing of the ear, but from what I have really handled and tasted and known for myself of the word of life—may I not say of that power of God unto salvation?" (I:365-6).

Elizabeth's influence extended itself far beyond the sphere of her personal exertions, and, in many places, both in this and other lands, her example of devotedness in the care of the wretched and vicious was emulated with blessed effect. At Petersburgh, the dowager empress adopted her plans and, most humanely, superintended the observance of them.

While thus animated by the evidence of a union of Christian effort, her spirit was often oppressed by many sorrows. Death visited the family circle, including her dear sister Priscilla, a devoted follower of Jesus, who was taken from the religious philanthropic service in which she had eminently adorned the cause of Christ. Elizabeth writes, "I feel brought low before the Lord. What can I say, and what can I do, but beseech Thee, O Lord! to care for us, present and absent; to undertake for us; to show us the sufficiency of thy grace, and the power of thy salvation? We beseech thee, through him that hath loved us and given himself for us, that thou wouldst draw us all, whether now far from thee, or near unto thee, by the powerful cords of thy loving-kindness, out of darkness into thy marvelous light; that we may ever dwell in thy love, and know the fullness of thy power, thy glory, and thy majesty. Amen" (I:407).

Early in 1824, Elizabeth paid another visit of Christian love to her friends. She returned home in feeble health. Shortly afterwards she entered the following lines in her journal, "Yesterday, after a very weak and faint morning, I attended our Ladies British Society meeting: it was surprising, even to myself, to find what had been accomplished. How many prisons are now visited and how much is done for the inhabitants of the prison-house, and what a way is made for their return from evil! It is marvelous, in my eyes, that a poor instrument should have been the apparent cause of setting forward such a work" (I:447). Elizabeth's reduced health now required entire relaxation, and she spent more than two months at Brighton. While there she was often distressed by the multitude of beggars who importuned her, and other visitors, for financial assistance. She earnestly desired that benevolent and wealthy persons, of whom there were many in Brighton, should form an association for inspecting and relieving the necessities of the sick and indigent. After much exertion and many discouragements she succeeded in organizing a District Visiting Society, which proved an instrument of service to many.

In the course of her illness at Brighton, she was frequently subject to faintness, and her attendants found it needful to place her at an open window for the refreshment of the air. On reviving from these attacks, one object always attracted her notice—the solitary Coast Guardsman. As she watched his measured steps, her interest became excited, and she ascertained that the service in which he was employed was one that entailed much privation, hardship, and danger. Her gentle spirit sympathized with him and his fellow-guardsmen, and she was anxious to promote their moral and religious improvement by supplying them with Bibles and other useful books. She applied to the committee of the Bible Society for a grant, which was liberally furnished. Fifty copies of the entire Bible and twenty-five New Testaments were promptly sent for her use. They were gratefully received, and there were afterwards evidences that they had been diligently and profitably read. On her return home, she wrote, "We left Brighton last Sixth-day; after what I passed through, in suffering and in doing, in various ways, I may acknowledge that I have no adequate expression to convey the gratitude due to my merciful and gracious Lord. I left it, after a stay of nearly ten weeks, with a comparatively healthy body, and, above all, with a remarkably clear and easy mind, with a portion of that overflowing peace that made all things, natural and spiritual, appear sweet" (I:461).

Some weeks afterwards she wrote, "I returned from a short expedition to Brighton last evening; a very interesting, and, I trust, not unimportant one. My object was the District Society that I was enabled to form there when I was so ill. Much good appears done; a fine arrangement made. I have not time to relate our interesting history, or how a poor unworthy woman, nothing extraordinary in point of power, simply seeking to follow a crucified Lord, and to cooperate with his grace in the heart, was yet followed after by almost every rank in society, with the greatest openness for any communications of a religious nature: William Allen was there, a great helper. Some of the poor blockade men seemed much affected by the attention paid to them, as also did their officers, and I am ready to hope that a little seed is scattered there" (I:462).

Shortly after her return to her own home, she felt constrained, through the influence of divine love, to undertake another and more extended mission—a visit to Ireland. In this, she was accompanied by her dear brother and helper, Joseph John Gurney, and her valued sister-in-law. A great variety of duties devolved upon them as they traveled through that country. In the principal cities and towns, particularly in Dublin, they were not only engaged in religious services amongst their friends, but large numbers of strangers attended the meetings at which they were present; and they also inspected prisons, asylums, bridewells,[8] houses of industry, etc.

Near the close of the arduous engagement, Elizabeth's health became seriously affected. Fever of a low character prostrated all her bodily energies. "I was," she says, "in one of my distressing faint states—tried without—feeling, such fears, lest my being thus stopped by illness should try the faith of others, and lest my own faith should fail—however, much as I suffered for a time, I had most sweet peace afterwards; my blessed Savior arose 'with healing in his wings,' delivered me from all my fears, and granted me such a sense of having obtained full reconciliation with my God, as I can hardly describe. I no longer hankered after home, but was able to commit myself, and those dearest to me, to this un-slumbering, all-merciful, and all-powerful shepherd" (I:520).

She was able to recover sufficiently to finish her labors in Ireland satisfactorily, and return home in safety and peace. But very soon the scene was changed—a heavy cloud was gathering round her and the beloved ones of her family circle. Her sister, Rachel Gurney, endeared to her by the closest bond of sisterhood, was seriously declining in health. Elizabeth passed some weeks at Brighton, tenderly nursing this dear invalid. During her stay she had a meeting with the members of the District Society, which, she says, "was humbling to me, as such exposures always are, more or less, and a real effort of duty, but I desired only to do it as such. Nothing of the kind appears to me to effect so much, as forming and helping these public charities, because so many are assisted by them. I also called at one of the Blockade Service stations, and found that the libraries, which I had sent three years ago, continued to be very useful to the men and their families. Out of deep distress I formed these institutions; surely out of weakness I was made strong. I was enabled to attend to my beloved sister during the remainder of her stay at Brighton, and then brought her home here; she left us for Earlham on Second day" (II:3).

A few weeks later Elizabeth visited Earlham to attend the dying bed of this excellent person. In the autumn of 1828, she wrote in her journal, "Dearest Lord! increase my faith more firmly; more fixedly establish me upon the Rock of Ages; that however the winds blow, the rains descend, or the floods beat against me, I may not be greatly moved: and let not any of the hindering or polluting things of this world lessen my love to thee, and to thy cause; or prevent my following hard after thee in spirit, with a humble, faithful, watchful, circumspect, and devoted heart" (II:29).

A short time elapsed after the last entry, ere (in consequence of the failure of one of the houses of business with which her husband was connected) the storm of worldly distress and perplexity was permitted to assail her, and severely to test the stability of her spiritual building. But it was, according to her fervent petition, firmly established on the Rock of Ages, Christ Jesus; and, though deeply conflicted in spirit, and suffering much from impaired bodily vigor, she was not overwhelmed. She besought her heavenly Father for "grace sufficient in this most awful time" (II:33), and truly his merciful ear was open to her prayer, and he enabled her, through the abundant outpouring of his Holy Spirit, to glorify him in the midst of the furnace of adversity, and to testify, from heartfelt and deeply-proved experience, that "the Lord is good, a stronghold in the day of trouble, and he knoweth them that trust in him" (Nah. 1:7).

She passed much of this season of sorrow in retirement and meditation, and derived great consolation from the records of divine inspiration; and having often witnessed the blessed influence which the sacred truths of Holy Scripture had produced on the minds of her fellow-believers in varied ranks of life, she was induced to select from its pages a portion for every day in the year. This little text book has been widely circulated, not only in this country, but also in many parts of the continent of Europe, and it continues to be a cherished and instructive memento of this devout servant of Christ.

Notwithstanding that many circumstances threatened to obstruct the prosecution of her important Christian labors; and for a time they were much restricted; some objects of special interest, which she had for a considerable time believed it to be her duty to accomplish, were still frequently presented to her mind, as a portion of that work in the vineyard of her Lord, which he had called her to perform. When natural feeling was disposed to shrink from further public engagement, she sought to commit her way unto him, and she says, in a letter to an absent daughter, "I have found such help and strength in prayer to God. . . . I think I have frequently, if not generally, come to be able to say, 'Not as I will, but as thou wilt'" (II:34).

Under date Eighth month, 29th, 1829, we find the following striking entry, "Our wedding day!—twenty-nine years since we married. My texts for the morning are applicable, 'Our light affliction, which is but for a moment, worketh for us a far more exceeding and eternal weight of glory' (2 Cor. 4:17). 'We walk by faith, not by sight' (2 Cor. 5:7). As far as we can judge from external appearances, mine has not been a common life. He who seeth in secret, only knows the unutterable depths and sorrows I have had to pass through, as well as, at other times, I may almost say, joys inexpressible and full of glory" (II:56).

The sympathy of her friends, of every class and denomination, had been powerfully excited, and she received, through various channels, the evidences of their high esteem, and also of their deep unity with her Christian efforts for the relief of human suffering, and the promotion of true religion in the souls of men: and many, who could correctly estimate the value of her services, strongly encouraged her to resume them. Her brothers were so fully impressed with the importance of sustaining her efforts for the welfare of her fellow-mortals, that they with a liberal hand supplied the resources which, during the remainder of her life, were required for the prosecution of her philanthropic labors, and for her subsequent travels in foreign parts.

About this time, accompanied by William Allen, she visited the Duchess of Kent and the Princess Victoria; and she writes, "We were received with much kindness and cordiality; and I felt my way open to express, not only my desire that the best blessing might rest upon them, but that the young princess might follow the example of our blessed Lord; that, as she grew in stature, she might grow in favor with God and man. I also ventured to remind her of King Josiah, who began to reign at eight years of age, and did that which was right in the sight of the Lord, turning neither to the right hand, nor to the left: which seemed to be well received" (II:86). An invitation was sent to Elizabeth by the Duchess of Gloucester, and, in reference to some religious communication with the duke and duchess, she says, "May good result to them, and no harm to myself; but I feel these openings a weighty responsibility, and desire to be faithful, not forward" (II:86).

In 1833 we find her first in Jersey, visiting in Christian love, the few Friends there, endeavoring to remedy the evils of the prison, the hospital, the workhouse, and lunatic asylum. We find her next in Guernsey, establishing The St. Peter's Port Provident and District Society, which at the present time is spoken of as having proved "a real blessing to the poor of the community" (II:134).

In the metropolis, Elizabeth's labors could be safely relaxed, all the prisons being placed under the care of efficient committees of the Ladies' British Society, and the impulse of heavenly love drew her into other fields of service for the welfare of her fellow-beings. Visiting the Isle of Wight, she was much interested in the condition of the Coast Guardsmen. Interviews with them stimulated her to undertake that great work of providing libraries for all the Coast Guard stations in Great Britain. Such an engagement presented great difficulties, and, to an ordinary mind, they would have appeared insurmountable, but it was a remarkable feature in the character of this gifted woman, that when an object of duty was clearly presented to her mind, no discouragement deterred her from pursuing it. She labored on with a quiet, patient perseverance until she saw it accomplished. Referring to the plan which she had projected, she afterwards says, "I have been very busy, trying to obtain libraries for all the Coast Guard stations, and have had to see men in authority, who received me in a way that was surprising to myself" (II:150).

The government sanctioned and assisted her efforts and, eventually, upwards of 52,400 volumes were provided for 600 libraries. But all this was not affected without much toil, a great deal of writing, many wearisome journeys to London, and the exercise of a rare degree of sound wisdom and discretion in the selection of the books suited to the purpose designed. Thus this vast undertaking, which, she says, she had "long had at heart," was accomplished to her great satisfaction; and she records her emotions as follows: "My desire is to do all these things with a single eye to the glory of God and the welfare of my fellow-mortals, and, if they succeed, to pray that he, who alone can bless and increase, may prosper the work of my unworthy hands; and that I may ever wholly give the glory to him to whom it is due" (II:165).

Before the close of 1835, she successfully made the further effort of supplying government and other packets, with libraries, containing a good supply of Bibles, Testaments, etc.; she also established one at Amesbury, for the use of the shepherds of Salisbury Plain. She afterwards received a great number of letters, all expressing gratitude and pleasure from the guardsmen and their officers, and she had as she remarks, "many proofs of the use and value of the libraries sent to them, proving it not to have been labor in vain in the Lord" (II:184-5).

Queries for Chapter Six

Consider, reflect on, and/or discuss the following queries:

1. Who assisted Elizabeth by taking over most of the duties related to the ministry to her poor neighbors and her school? Have you experienced a time in your life when you had to give some of your responsibilities to others? How did you feel? Did you immediately go into another area of service?

2. How did Elizabeth respond to the death of the little boy who did not have money for food or lodging? How have you responded to the needs of the homeless and hungry in your area? What other ways can you help?

3. What ministry was an outgrowth of Elizabeth's time at Brighton recovering from illness? Have you had an experience of turning a difficult time into an opportunity for service?

4. Traveling adversely affected Elizabeth's health, yet she continued to minister. Was this a wise decision? Would you continue to do something that made you sick? Where did her strength come from? Do you think she could have taken better care of herself while traveling and ministering?

5. Is there any incongruity between Elizabeth's ministry to the Coast Guard and the Friends' Peace Testimony? Explain why or why not.

Chapter Seven

Traveling Ministry

Elizabeth visited the Channel Islands during the summer of 1836. A variety of important engagements awaited her while on this excursion. Both then, and on many subsequent occasions, she was employed in forming district societies, as well as organizing committees for the care of prisons, hospitals, and houses of correction.

In First month, 1838, with the cordial approval of her friends, and furnished by the meetings with which she was in connection with credentials testifying their full unity with her proposed services, Elizabeth commenced a series of visits to various nations of the European continent. In the first, she was accompanied by her husband and their valued friend Josiah Forster. The formalities of introduction were little needed to bring her into association with a great variety of serious persons, who knew that the objects which induced her to undertake these journeys were widely different from those that usually attract visitors to foreign lands. She went not in the pursuit of health, worldly gain, or self-gratification, but in obedience to an impulse which she certainly believed to be divine; she sought to follow the voice that called her, and the guidance of an unerring hand. It led her to explore the abodes of sorrow, of suffering, and of vice, where, with a wonderful degree of skill and energy, she suggested plans of amelioration and reform.

Assisted by excellent individuals, whose hearts were influenced by a measure of that love and zeal which animated her own spirit, her efforts were remarkably crowned with success. But it was not only in the interests of suffering humanity that she was welcomed wherever she went as a sister beloved in the Lord. Her company was desired, and her pious exhortations and devout prayers made a deep impression on persons of every rank.

Those who, from their exalted position, are rarely accessible to such as occupy a private station in life, sought interviews with this messenger of truth. Sovereign princes and royal nobles received, with seriousness and affectionate respect, the admonitory sentiment, or the word that stimulated to the performance of duty. The accents of sympathy and the language of encouragement conveyed a soothing balm to the sorrowing hearts of some who, while surrounded by earthly splendor, were no strangers to the vicissitudes and afflictions that attend our mortal being. The distinction between their external circumstances and those of this devoted Christian philanthropist was no barrier against the emotions of friendship and high esteem. Many had heard, and some had witnessed, that she was endowed, through the power of the Holy Spirit, with gifts of priceless value, compared with which, all worldly grandeur sinks into insignificance. There were, amongst the varied classes of the people, some who were prepared to participate with her in the overflowing of that stream of heavenly love which, springing from the abounding grace of God, ennobles its possessor with the riches of faith—the heirship of a kingdom infinite in glory, and eternal in duration.

In Paris, which was the chief scene of her first benevolent exertions on the continent, she and her companions inspected prisons, hospitals, schools, etc. Many other important objects claimed their attention. There were, in that city, kindred hearts who rendered efficient assistance to the visitors; and some excellent ladies, devoted to the cause of the redeemer, whose light shone brightly amidst much surrounding darkness, became united to Elizabeth in the bonds of cordial affection and true gospel fellowship. She addressed most solemn and impressive exhortations to poor prisoners on the circumstances of the prodigal son, a French lady having read the parable. Afterwards she visited the king (Louis Philippe), his queen, and Princess Adelaide, strongly expressing to the queen a desire for a more extended reading of the Scriptures and better observance of the Sabbath.

Then she proceeded to the residence of the youthful Duchess of Orleans, the bereaved widow of the heir apparent to the throne of France. "[T]here," says Elizabeth, "we had a delightful visit—the sweetest religious communication with her; and other interesting conversation" (II:237). The fatigue to which Elizabeth was subjected was often very great, but she records the thankful acknowledgment, "He who I believe put me forth has, from season to season, restored my soul and body, and helped me from hour to hour. I have exceedingly and deeply felt my utter unworthiness, and that all is from the fullness and freeness of unmerited mercy and love, in Christ Jesus" (II:239).

Shortly after their return to London, the following entry occurs in the journal: "Yesterday was the largest British Society meeting I ever remember; partly collected to hear my account of our French journey. There must have been some hundreds present; many of them ladies of rank. My prayers have arisen that, however imperfectly or unworthily sown, the seed scattered yesterday may be so prospered by the Lord's power, life, and grace, that it may bear a full crop to his praise" (II:241). In Eighth month, Elizabeth, with the approval of her friends, again visited the meetings of her own religious Society in Scotland, having also many opportunities of declaring the blessed truths of the gospel of Christ to large congregations of varied classes of Christian believers. She also effected some very important improvements in the care of several prisons, finding others "in excellent order"—the happy consequence of her previous regulations (II:247).

Early in the succeeding year [1839], we find her again at Paris, with her husband, her eldest daughter, and their former kind companion, Josiah Forster. Much important service awaited her, both in that city and many other places in France, also in the principal towns of Switzerland. At the commencement of this engagement, she wrote as follows: "How earnestly do I desire and pray that my Lord would clearly point out my work, and enable me, by his power and Spirit, to perform it to his praise, the good of others, and my own peace! Lord, regard thy servant in her low estate; and, if it be thy holy will, give some token, by thy presence, Spirit, and power, that thou art with us, and more abundantly fit and prepare for thine own work.

I beseech thee to give thy poor servant a quiet, patient, trustful mind; only dependent upon the fresh puttings forth of thy Spirit, and the incomings of thy love. Amen" (II:266).

Her gospel ministrations, throughout this extensive journey, were described as being of a powerfully impressive and instructive character. She visited many persons who filled conspicuous and important stations in life, to whom her influence was evidently blessed. She also addressed the wretched inmates of the prisons in the awakening strains of gospel invitation. While in Paris, a large company passed an evening with her and her companions, more than a hundred persons consisting of different classes and religious groups including Catholics, Protestants, and some of the Greek Church. In this remarkable assemblage were Greeks, Ionians, Spaniards, a Pole, Italians, Germans, English, Americans, and French. Elizabeth, in writing some account of the opportunity, says, "There was a sweet feeling of the love of God over us. We finished by reading, in a solemn manner, the fifteenth of Luke: I made a little comment—there was very great solemnity" (II:273).

Of another occasion she writes, "Our great philanthropic evening was largely attended. I strongly impressed the extreme importance of the influence of the higher on the lower classes of society, by their example and precept; mentioned late hours, theatres, and other evils. Then advised giving the poor: Christian education, lending libraries, district societies, and other objects. We finished with a very solemn Scripture reading, third chapter of Colossians, and the twentieth and twenty-first verses of the last chapter of Hebrews. I expressed some solemn parting truths, and our party broke up in much love and peace" (II:274).

Services of a similar character fell to her lot in many places during their travels, and among the interests of the present mission, few afforded more satisfaction than a visit to their fellow Quakers, the Friends of Congenies and its vicinity. In reference to it, Elizabeth wrote, "I humbly trust that the blessing of the Lord was with us; I have seldom felt more peace than when engaged in these labors of Christian love at Congenies, or more clear belief that I was in my right place" (II:294).

After their return home, some religious engagements of a very important nature claimed her attention, both amongst the members of her own Christian community and in a more extended sphere. In company with her brother, Samuel Gurney, and their friend, William Allen, she by appointment visited their youthful queen, and expressed words of encouragement in the pursuit of virtue, and of "desire that the blessing of God might rest upon the queen and her consort" (II:336).

Her two companions in this interview became, a few weeks later, united with her in another journey on the continent. The travelers proceeded to Belgium, having much weighty service, particularly in Brussels. They had an interesting conversation with the king, introducing various subjects of great importance, to which he gave the kindest attention. Elizabeth pleaded successfully with the amiable Queen of Hanover for a remission of the sufferings of prisoners, and enforced the importance of circulating the Holy Scriptures. In Prussia, her benevolent and Christian efforts were cordially encouraged by several members of the reigning family, particularly by the king's sister, an eminently pious and devoted lady. The crown prince also received the visitors with much kindness. While in Berlin, an excellent address was presented to the king containing a respectful, but earnest, remonstrance on behalf of a body of Lutheran professors, who, through conscientiously dissenting from the national church, were subjected to imprisonment. It was well received, the king saying he thought "the Spirit of God must have helped them to express themselves as they had done." At Minden and Pyrmont, the travelers spent some days in sweet Christian communion with a number of valuable persons, members of the Society of Friends, to whom their visit was edifying and comforting. They returned home in much peace.

In retrospect of the journey, Elizabeth's mind dwelt on an excellent establishment which she had witnessed at Kaisersworth, near Dusseldorf, at which serious-minded young women were trained to fill the responsible situation of nurses to the sick. She saw the great advantage that would result from a similar institution in her own land, and with her typical energy and wisdom, she organized a committee which commenced the undertaking. The institution has steadily advanced and prospered, the aid of the

Nursing Sisters having been sought and greatly prized by persons of every rank, not excepting members of the royal family.

One more lengthened journey on the continent appeared to the mind of this devoted gospel messenger, to be called for by her divine master. She felt strongly attracted by the constraining love of Christ to visit those who desired to serve his holy cause of righteousness and mercy, in the kingdoms of Holland, Denmark, Prussia, and other German states. Her beloved brother, Joseph John Gurney, united with her in this gospel mission. They landed at Rotterdam, where they had a large meeting for worship and visited prisons there and at Gouda, having much satisfaction in these engagements. On arriving at Hague, they received an early invitation to visit the king, queen, and Princess Sophia. With these very interesting persons they had a remarkable interview.

Elizabeth says: "We all felt very weightily our serious engagement. The king began easy and pleasant conversation with me about my visiting prisons. I told him, in a short, lively manner, the history of it. He appeared much interested, as did the queen. I then said, my brother had visited the West Indies and would be glad to tell the king and queen the result of his observations in those islands. This he did capitally; he represented also the sad effects of the Dutch enlisting soldiers on the Gold Coast (in Africa), and how it led to evil and slavery; which so touched the king, that he said he meant to put a stop to it. I then most seriously laid before the king the sad defect of having no religious education in their government schools, and the Bible not introduced. I expressed my desire that the blessing of the Almighty might rest on the king, queen, their children, and their children's children. The king then took me by the hand, and said he hoped God would bless me. We gave them books, which they accepted kindly" (II:389-90).

The travelers also visited several other members of this royal family—all excellent persons—with whom they had very important communication on many points. They then proceeded to Amsterdam and Bremen. At the latter place they had a large public meeting for worship. Long before the appointed hour, well-dressed persons entered the noble building to secure places. Several pastors were present. One of them, at the close, addressed the missionary brother and sister, expressing his desire that what had been uttered might be blessed to the people, and that they might be themselves blessed. To Elizabeth he said, "Your name has long been to us a word of beauty." A Christian gentleman, in a note to her and her brother, remarked, "No, I am more than convinced that you are sent to us by the Lord, to become a great blessing, and a salt to our city" (II:391).

After similar services at Hamburg, they crossed the Baltic to Copenhagen, and on the morning after their arrival, the Queen of Denmark came from her country palace, ten miles distant, to welcome the visitors, and to take Elizabeth in her carriage to her infant school. "It was," says Elizabeth, "really beautiful to see her surrounded by the little children, and to hear her translating what I wished to say to them" (II:400).

In the evening they drove to the palace, and were invited by the king and queen to dine there a few days later, when the inspection of the prisons might be completed. This was, Elizabeth says, "a very serious occasion; as we had so much to lay before the king—slavery in the West Indies, the condition of the prisons, etc. I was, in spirit, so weighed down with the importance of the occasion, that I could hardly enjoy the beautiful scene. The queen met us with the utmost kindness and condescension, and took us a walk in their lovely grounds. The king also met us very courteously. After dinner the king and queen took us to the drawing room window to see a large school of orphans, protégés of the queen" (II:401).

These children had been brought from the city in twenty-five carts to enjoy a holiday, and, as the queen said, "to meet Madame Fry." How interesting was this arrangement of the excellent queen; so calculated to fix, in the remembrance of the infantile group, the person and character of this eminent Christian philanthropist, and to sow, in their youthful bosoms, a seed of benevolence and virtue, that might in due season produce a fruit; partaking of the nature of that influence from which it originated. A shower of rain coming, the king and queen had all the orphans collected around them in the salon. This afforded an opportunity for a religious communication from Elizabeth, which was interpreted by a German prince, who was so impressed by the sweetness and power of her ministry, that, in the midst of his interpretation, he exclaimed, "C'est un don de Dieu!" (It is a gift from God!)

A few days subsequent to this remarkable occasion, the travelers paid another visit to the king and queen at their country palace, and had much interesting communication with them. Elizabeth read a portion of Scripture, and expressed her "religious concern and desires" for the best welfare of the royal pair whose kindness, she says, was very great. Before quitting Copenhagen she had "a most delightful farewell religious opportunity" (II:403) with the queen and princess. She also paid a very interesting visit to the dowager-queen and another to the prince and princess of Hesse Cassel.

In reviewing their engagements, she says, "I believe we were sent to Copenhagen for a purpose. May our unworthy labors be blessed to the liberation of many captives, spiritually and temporally" (II:403). Returning to Hamburg, they proceeded to Pyrmont and Minden, where they were refreshed and comforted by meetings with their own religious community, also by a very satisfactory one at Buckeberg, where many of the higher rank, including the reigning prince and princesses of a German state, were assembled. Thence they went forward to Hanover, visiting on their route the great prison at Hameln, where the chains that had heavily fettered a vast number of poor prisoners had been removed in consequence of the intercession of the late, excellent Queen of Hanover, who was stimulated to this merciful intervention by the influence of Elizabeth Gurney Fry.

In Prussia and Silesia, they had much religious interaction with a large circle of truly Christian princes and nobles, and were welcomed by the king and queen with the most kind and cordial friendship. In a large assemblage of persons of the poorer class were mingled twelve of the royal family, with other princes and princesses and nobles, all listening with devout attention to the solemn and impressive ministrations of their visitors. One who was present says of Elizabeth's address that "with her usual clearness and power, each individual, each class present, seemed included. Never did she address any assembly more beautifully, with more unction, or more truly from the depths of her heart; and no audience could have given more profound attention to every word she uttered" (II:415). From Berlin she returned home; suffering much from fatigue; and her health became now seriously enfeebled, but she received the dispensation with a meek and patient spirit.

At the commencement of the following year, 1842, her accustomed vigor continued to decline, but the fervency of her zeal to procure relief to suffering fellow-creatures was undiminished; and, on a public occasion, she availed herself of an opportunity to plead with some of the rulers of her own nation, for several important measures of amelioration and reform. The King of Prussia visited the English court shortly after, and, by his particular request, Elizabeth met him at the Mansion House and had with him "much deeply interesting conversation on various important subjects of mutual interest" (II:434).

The king arranged to meet Elizabeth at the Newgate prison. It was a memorable occasion. The female prisoners were seated on each side of a lengthened row of tables. They were neatly clad, their conduct and manner was orderly and respectful, and although surrounded by much that was calculated to excite their curiosity and to attract their gaze, not one was observed to look around at the strangers present. The king led Elizabeth to a chair at the head of the table and sat beside her. A considerable number of persons were arranged around the large room, including some noblemen, English and foreign; city authorities, in their scarlet robes of office; and many ladies, including members of the prison committee. Yet, notwithstanding that the assembled company was of so unusual a character, it did not distract the attention of the poor prisoners. They appeared to listen with seriousness to the chapter and psalm which were read by Elizabeth, and to an impressive address and prayer which she offered at the conclusion. How wonderful was the contrast between the solemnity and the deep stillness that pervaded the apartment, and the riotous and savage turbulence which formerly reigned there!

On the eighth of the following Fifth month, Elizabeth entered in her journal, "On Third day the lady mayoress and I paid interesting and satisfactory visits to the queen dowager, the Duchess of Kent, and the Duchess of Gloucester. I went with my heart lifted up for help, and strength, and direction, that the visits might prove useful, and that I might drop the word in season; and that I might myself be kept humble, watchful, and faithful to my Lord. With the queen dowager, and her sister, the Duchess of Saxe Weimar, etc., we had a very satisfactory time, much lively and edifying conversation. With the Duchess of Kent, had interesting conversation about our dear young queen, Prince Albert, and their little ones. I desired, wherever I could, to throw in a hint of a spiritual kind, and was enabled to do it. I gave the duchess some papers; with a note to Prince Albert, requesting him to lay the suffering state of the Waldenses, from their fresh persecutions, before the queen" (II:440).

A few months later, we find Elizabeth receiving a letter from Kamehameha III, King of the Sandwich Islands. He too had heard of the universality of her Christian interest in the welfare of mankind. His people were, through the avarice of Europeans, largely supplied with ardent spirits, which caused sickness, poverty, and crime to prevail among them. He sought the kind intervention of this philanthropist, that the importation of these harmful beverages might be prevented. Elizabeth pleaded the cause of these islanders with the first minister of state in a neighboring country. Thus, from the appeal of suffering, or the plaint of woe, she could not turn away her ear; but, from whatever portion of the habitable globe it might arise, the heaven-inspired compassion which actuated her, impelled her to seek a remedy for the evil.

But while with unremitting energy she sought to pour a healing balm into the wounds of sin and sorrow which so largely pervade the ranks of human society, this devoted servant of God was permitted to partake, in no small degree, of the afflictions incident to this probationary state. Her health so evidently declined as to induce her family to promote her residence for some months at Cromer, where she might obtain both rest and invigorating air. She reluctantly quitted, for a time, her sphere of active exertion. She writes, "I have sought to have my steps directed by him who knows what is best for us" (II:441), and, after alluding to her failing strength, she adds, "not that I fear for the everlasting state, although this confidence arises from no trust in anything in myself, but faith in the mercy of God in Christ, who tasted death for every man, and a full belief that, unworthy as I am, through his mercy he will not cast me out of his presence (which I delight in), nor shut up his tender mercies from me" (II:441).

In her retirement at Cromer, however, she followed the impulse of duty by undertaking to establish a library and reading room for the fishermen, as well as a Friendly Society for their temporal aid. She was, as she says, encouraged in wakeful hours of the night by these words, "steadfast, immovable, always abounding in the work of the Lord. In weakness and in strength we must, as ability is granted, abound in the work of the Lord. May our labor not be in vain in him" (1 Cor. 15:58).

As the spring returned, she felt strongly attracted to pay, once more, a short visit to some dear Christian friends at Paris, who were her helpers in those works of mercy which had already occupied her attention in that city. In Fourth month she went thither, in company with her brother, Joseph John, and his wife. Her heart was gladdened by a renewal of association with devoted servants of the Lord Jesus, who, amidst the dissipation and irreligion of a great metropolis, were as "the salt of the earth," and who, she says, "have been greatly prospered in their work of Christian love, in which they have persevered ever since my first visit to Paris" (II:469).

She again, by appointment, visited the king, queen, and Princess Adelaide, and had a long and deeply interesting interview with the Duchess of Orleans and her step-mother, the Grand Duchess of Mecklenburgh, on which occasion the interaction was of a most instructive character. She returned home, with a peaceful and encouraged spirit, attended some of the sittings of the Yearly Meeting of Friends, and afterwards the annual convention of the British Ladies' Society.

As the summer advanced, her health appeared to be fast declining. The autumn was passed at Sandgate and Tonbridge Wells, but these changes failed to invigorate her enfeebled frame. During the ensuing winter, her physical suffering was intense, but while enduring agonizing pain, she said that the everlasting arms were underneath—that the undercurrent was peaceful, notwithstanding that the surface was so greatly tempest-tossed. In her journal she entered the prayer, "Most gracious Lord! may it please thee to grant me grace, minute by minute, to hold fast my confidence steadfast unto the end; that, continuing faithful unto death, I may, through thy merits, receive a crown of life" (II:478).

On the return of spring in the following year, 1844, there was some perceptible improvement in her health. Her justly-valued brother-in-law, Sir T.F. Buxton, whose bodily state had become greatly reduced by lengthened illness, was removed to Bath for the benefit of the waters and the warmer air. Elizabeth had a strong desire that the same means of restoration might be rendered available to herself, and also that she might be located, for a time, in the vicinity of her much-loved sister Buxton. With no small difficulty her removal to Bath was accomplished. Her stay there was a source of mutual solace to each of the afflicted parties, and she returned home early in the summer with a considerable accession of strength. But he "whose ways are not as our ways" (Isa. 55:8-9) saw fit, in his inscrutable wisdom, to prove her faith by yet deeper trials, removing from her family circle several of its most cherished members, permitting the scythe of death, to cut down the aged, those also of infantile years and of youthful promise, together with some in the vigor of life.

In Seventh month, her dear sister-in-law, for many years her companion and fellow-laborer in the gospel of Christ, finished her earthly course in peace and joy. A darling grandson was consigned to the grave; and, during the succeeding month, her son, William—the stay and succor of his suffering and sorrowing mother—with two of his lovely daughters, were, within a few days of each other, numbered with the inhabitants of the invisible world.

Recounting the distressful events that marked this awful dispensation, Elizabeth wrote, "O, dear Lord! keep thy unworthy and poor, sick servant, in this time of unutterable trial—bless and sanctify to us all, this affliction, and cause it to work for our everlasting good: and be very near to the poor, dear widow and fatherless; and may we all be drawn nearer to thee, and thy kingdom of rest and peace" (II:500).

Her last written communication to the committee of the British Ladies' Society was a touching, and truly Christian salutation; concluding, "May the Holy Spirit of God direct your steps, strengthen your hearts, and enable you and me to glorify our holy head, in doing and suffering, even unto the end; and when the end comes, through a Savior's love and merits, may we be received into glory and everlasting peace" (II:504).

One month more brought additional bereavements. A lovely niece, with her infant son, were taken from the mourning circle, then a few weeks later, her beloved brother, Buxton, closed his honorable earthly course. When daily anticipating the announcement of the solemn event, she wrote to his eldest daughter, "May our afflictions be sanctified to us; not leading us to the world for consolation, but more fully to cast ourselves on him who died for us, and hath loved us with an everlasting love" (II:507).

Queries for Chapter Seven

Consider, reflect on, and/or discuss the following queries:

1. Reflect on Elizabeth's numerous journeys to the European continent. What was their purpose? What did they accomplish?

2. Elizabeth moved easily amongst the poor but also amongst nobility. Why was this important? Are you intimidated by famous/noble persons? Would you feel comfortable sharing your faith with the rich and the poor?

3. How does Elizabeth keep from being conceited in regards to all her accomplishments? Do you give God the glory for all you accomplish in life?

4. Where does Elizabeth say she knew she was in the "right place" for her? Why? Have you ever felt that way?

5. A Christian gentleman said Elizabeth and Joseph John were a "salt to our city." What did he mean? Where does the Bible talk about salt in a similar way?

6. What great sorrows did Elizabeth experience during this time and how did she deal with those? How do you deal with the great sorrows in your life?

Chapter Eight

The Final Year

Elizabeth felt a strong desire once more to visit the home of her youth, and to partake of the solace that tenderly-endeared family affection supplies to the sorrowing heart. The journey to Earlham was undertaken early in the spring of 1845. She spent many weeks there and at Northrepps. Association with her beloved relatives, and the sympathy with her widowed sister Buxton (deeply impressed as it was by the communion of affliction), was a source of mutual consolation to their stricken, but submissive spirits. Elizabeth now frequently attended the meetings of Friends in Norwich, ministering with remarkable power and life to those who were assembled there.

On her return home she was twice present at the Yearly Meeting of her own Religious Society in London. On both occasions she addressed the large congregation with much solemnity and appropriateness, and at the close of her last communication she offered, in sublime, impressive language, a fervent prayer and ascription of praise to him whom she had long loved and served.

A few days afterwards she met her faithful friends and fellow-laborers of the British Ladies' Society, on the occasion of their annual meeting, which, to accommodate her, was held at Plaistow. Her great feebleness affected them with sorrow, but they were tenderly interested in once more communing with this revered and beloved servant of God.

As the summer advanced, her family members were anxious that she should partake of the invigorating influence of sea air, and a suitable house at Ramsgate was prepared for her. On being settled there, she wrote, "It still pleases my heavenly Father that afflictions should abound to me in this tabernacle. Lord! through the fullness of thy love and pity and unmerited mercy, be pleased to arise for my help; bind up my broken heart, heal my wounded spirit, and yet enable thy servant, through the power of thy own Spirit, in everything to return thee thanks; and not to faint in the day of trouble; but, in humility and godly fear, to show forth thy praise" (II:523). About two weeks later, she penned some lines to her brother, Samuel Gurney, in which, after saying that she committed body, soul, and spirit, to the gracious care of her Lord, she added, "I have the humble trust that he will be my keeper, even unto the end; and when the end comes, through the fullness of his love and the abundance of his merits, I shall join those who, after having passed through great tribulation, are forever at rest in Jesus, having 'washed their robes and made them white in the blood of the Lamb'" (II:524). Her physical powers continued to decline; yet that flame of heavenly love which had so long glowed within her heart could not be extinguished by suffering or by sorrow; and she employed her little remaining strength in circulating, amongst the seamen at Ramsgate, copies of the Holy Scriptures, and, amongst the poor and the laborers whom she saw in her rides, some tracts to stimulate them to love and fear their creator.

For several successive weeks she attended the small Meeting for Worship of Friends at Drapers, four miles from Ramsgate. Her engagements in the ministry of the gospel are described as having been, on these occasions, very solemn and instructive. On the first day preceding that on which she died, her communication was remarked as being most impressively striking to all present. She afterwards repeatedly alluded to the opportunity, as having been one in which the divine presence had been signally vouchsafed. She said, "We have had a very remarkable meeting—such a peculiarly solemn time" (II:527). She had then, unconsciously, finished her public labors. In the private circle, the entire absence of choice or will in connection with temporal things indicated her near approach to those of eternal duration. On the day which preceded the final seizure, she was employed in transcribing, at the request of a friend who desired her autograph, some texts from the New Testament. She chose passages which declare the universality of the love of God through Jesus Christ. What theme could more befit the last reflection of those rays of light, by which, from her youthful days, the "Son of Righteousness" had illumined her soul? She had experientially known the guiding and sustaining influence of this redeeming love. She had witnessed its power to soften the obdurate heart, to attract the worldly, and to reclaim the prodigal. Now, as she was treading the final step that intervened between the sanctified spirit and the region of light and joy, she left her dying testimony to the blessedness of this fathomless love. The selections were accompanied by this short note, the last effort of her pen, "I have copied for thee these valuable texts, that prove salvation is open to all (through a Savior's love and merits) who believe in him; who no longer live unto themselves, but unto him who died for them, and rose again" (II:530).

In the evening of the following day, the eleventh of Tenth month, she became suddenly affected with some paralytic symptoms. She said to her attendant, "Oh! Mary, dear Mary, I am very ill!" After an affectionate response from the faithful nurse, the dear sufferer added, "Pray for me! It is a strift, but I am safe." This was, indeed, the fearful "strift" of nature—the disruption of the mortal fabric—but its celestial tenant was, forever, "safe." A few hours afterwards, in a slow, distinct voice, the last utterance was heard, "Oh! my dear Lord, help and keep thy servant!" (II:534). Early on the succeeding morning, the thirteenth of Tenth month, 1845, her immortal spirit, kept by infinite power and love, winged its flight, as we may assuredly believe, to its mansion of glory in the heavenly Father's house.

Such was the close of a life eminently dedicated to the service of God; to follow the example which it sets before us must involve many a sacrifice of vain inclination and selfish desire. But how infinitely blessed is this course of Christian devotedness! How does the radiance of "the peace of God" (Col. 3:15) shine on the straight and narrow path, which Jesus assures us leads to life! And when the fleeting and uncertain period of earthly probation terminates, how is it recompensed by "joy unspeakable and full of glory" (1 Pet. 1:8).

Queries for Chapter Eight

Consider, reflect on, and/or discuss the following queries:

1. What type of ministry engaged Elizabeth's declining energies during her final year? Have you known others who have been actively serving in ministry right up to the time of their deaths?

2. How was Elizabeth received by her fellow members of the Society of Friends? How does your meeting receive and respond to the ministry of older members?

3. What efforts were made by the British Ladies' Society to enable her to participate in their annual meeting? How have you reached out to assist an older person in your meeting or community?

4. What type of ministry did Elizabeth engage in at Ramsgate, where she was sent for her health? Does such a ministry still have value today?

5. Where did Elizabeth attend meeting during her final days? Was she an active participant in the ministry there? Are you an active participant in your meeting, or just an attender?

6. What was Elizabeth's final act of ministry?

7. Consider and reflect upon the death of Elizabeth Gurney Fry in light of the life that she lived. What lessons are to be learned?

Notes

Introduction
[1] In Quaker terminology, the term "gathered meeting" indicates that Friends have gathered in one accord and have prepared their hearts and minds (called "centering down") so that they are open to hearing God's message.
[2] In Quaker usage a "convinced" Friend is one who comes from another religious body and chooses to accept Quaker beliefs and practices.

Chapter One
[3] Quakers often refer to the "light within," the "teacher within," or here, the "monitor within."

Chapter Two
[4] For Quakers, who do not traditionally practice water baptism, the baptism of significance is a spiritual baptism.
[5] Instead of using the pagan names (Sunday, Monday, etc.) for days of the week, Quakers speak of "First-day" (Sunday), "Second-day" (Monday), etc.

Chapter Three
[6] The language in Paul's epistle to the Corinthian church, forbidding the women to speak and ask questions in their congregations, has been much dwelt upon, as evidence that the public ministry of females is not admissible in Christian assemblies for worship: but such an application of the apostle's directions must involve a plain contradiction of his previous injunctions in the same epistle, where he describes the manner in which women should be attired, or should demean themselves, when publicly praying or prophesying. Those whom he commanded to "keep silence

in the church" could not be engaged in that exercise of prophecy which he had just before spoken of, as "speaking unto men, to edification, exhortation, and comfort."

Chapter Four
[7] One of the accomplices in this robbery, who confessed his guilt as the principal actor, declared uniformly, and to the last moments, the innocence of this young woman; her guilt was never proved.

Chapter Six
[8] Bridewell: a prison or reformatory.

Bibliography

A Brief Memoir of the Life of Elizabeth Fry. Philadelphia, 1858.

Adams, Elmer C., and Warren Dunham Foster. *Heroines of Modern Progress*.

Burton, Edwin. "Society for Promotion of Christian Knowledge." In *The Catholic Encyclopedia, Volume III*. Online Edition, 2003. New York: Robert Appleton Company, 1908. 6 July 2004. <http://www.newadvent.org/cathen/03720a.htm>.

Byron, Lord. "Don Juan." In *The Works of Lord Byron*. Hertfordshire: Wordsworth Poetry Library, 1994.

Corder, Susanna. *Life of Elizabeth Fry: Compiled from her journal, as edited by her daughters, and from various other sources*. Philadelphia: Henry Longstreth, 1855.

Fay, Elizabeth. *The Bluestocking Archive*. University of Massachusetts, Boston. 25 June 2004. < http://www.faculty.umb.edu/elizabeth_fay/archive2.html>.

Fry, Katharine, Rachel Elizabeth Cresswell, and Elizabeth Gurney Fry. *Memoir of the Life of Elizabeth Fry*. 2 vols. London, 1847. Earlham School of Religion, Digital Quaker Collection. < http://dqc.esr.earlham.edu>.

Goff, David. "Post-Millenial Optimism in Sarah Scott's *Millenium Hall*." In *South East Atlantic Society for Eighteenth Century Studies Conference*. 9 July 2004.

Hatton, Jean. *Betsy: The Dramatic Biography of Prison Reformer Elizabeth Fry*. Grand Rapids: Monarch, 2005.

Johnson, R. Brimley, ed. *Elizabeth Fry's Journeys on the Continent 1840-1841, From a Diary Kept by Her Niece Elizabeth Gurney*. Suffolk, Great Britain: Richard Clay & Sons, 1931.

Kelly, Gary. "Introduction: Sarah Scott, Bluestocking Feminism, and Millenium Hall." In *Millenium Hall*. Sarah Scott, author. Orchard Park, NY: Broadview, 1995. 11-46.

Mossman, Samuel. "Mrs. Elizabeth Fry: The Reformer of Female Prison Discipline." In *Gems of Womanhood; or, Sketches of Distinguished Women in Various Ages and Nations*. Edinburgh: Gall & Inglis, 1870.

Pitman, Mrs. E. R. *Elizabeth Fry*. 1886. Reprint. New York: Greenwood, 1969.

Rolka, Gail Meyer. "Elizabeth Fry." In *100 Women Who Shaped World History*. San Francisco: Bluewood, 1994.

Rose, June. *Elizabeth Fry...a Biography*. London: Macmillan, 1980.

Ryder, Edward. *Elizabeth Fry*. New York: 1884.

Skidmore, Gil., ed. *Elizabeth Fry: A Quaker Life, Selected Letters and Writings*. Lanham, MD: AltaMira, 2005.

Swift, David E. "Charles Simeon and J. J. Gurney: A Chapter in Anglican-Quaker Relations." In *Church History*. 29:2. (Jun 1960). 167-186. Carson-Newman College. 30 June 2007. <http://www.jstor.org>.

Symonds, Richard. *Far Above Rubies: The Women Uncommemorated by the Church of England*. Harrisburg, PA: Morehouse, 1993.

Whitney, Janet. *Elizabeth Fry, Quaker heroine*. Boston: Little, Brown, 1937.

Printed in the United States
202474BV00002B/1-159/P